MAR 3 0 1982

979.1
M

cop. 1

Measeles, Evelyn Brack

Lee's Ferry: A Crossing on the
Colorado

LEE'S FERRY

For Toni and Charles who first showed us the Southwest—
For Marjorie and Mr. Jack who love it so well—
But mostly for Robert
Who shared it with me.

Evelyn Brack Measeles
Santa Fe, New Mexico
1981

A Crossing on the Colorado

LEE'S FERRY

Evelyn
Brack
Measeles

PRUETT **P** PUBLISHING COMPANY
Boulder, Colorado

Library of Congress Cataloging in Publication Data

Measeles, Evelyn Brack, 1921-
   Lee's Ferry: a crossing on the Colorado.

   Bibliography: p.
   Includes index.
   1. Lees Ferry, Ariz.—History. 2. Lee, John Doyle,
1812-1877. 3. Mountain Meadows Massacre, 1857.
4. Mormons and Mormonism in Utah—Biography. I. Title.
F819.L44L435   979.1'302   80-28368
ISBN 0-87108-576-3 Cloth
ISBN 0-87108-592-5 Paper

First Edition

1 2 3 4 5 6 7 8 9

Printed in the United States of America

Acknowledgements

Some twenty-odd years ago we moved west to begin work with the Bureau of Indian Affairs and were temporarily assigned to Holbrook, Arizona. We ended up living in the country, at a place "way out" on McLaw's Road where we rented a house from the people for whom the road was named.

With the wide expanse, the mesas, the Indians, the residents of this small town, we felt at home. Living in the midst of Mormon Country and feeling we would, somehow, be associated with the Southwest forevermore, we began to read about the land and the people with whom we would share it. The "Old Man" John McLaws, (a somewhat respectful sobriquet the townspeople had given him), told me he was the first white child born on the Little Colorado and that in coming to this place, his family had crossed at Lee Ferry. It was thus that I was initiated early into the different ways people prefer to say that name or write it down, and thus began my odyssey with the ferry.

This slim volume is the result of many happy hours of reading where, whenever I would come across something about that place, it would become a FILE item.

For many years my source was the Arizona State Library, which mailed copies of books to me at Canyon de Chelly, Navajo Reservation, Chinle, Arizona. Occasionally I got books from the Gallup Public Library.

Out of that ever-expanding FILE, with some of my own words and many quoted from others, I have made, hopefully, a story of Lee's Ferry.

Though I know none personally, I am indebted to and have an authorial affection for all of those listed in the bibliography; those who have studied the river. I am especially grateful to Juanita Brooks, who has written so often and so compellingly of Lee, and to her coeditor of the *Diaries,* Robert Glass Cleland. One is also in the debt of the historians of the river: C. Gregory Crampton, Frederick Dellenbaugh, Leland Hargrave Creer, Dwight Smith; to those who edited and footnoted the journals—Herbert E. Gregory, Charles Kelly, William Culp Darrah; and researchers who cared about those who went through the canyons, and how they went through, or if they got through at all—writers like Otis Marston, W.L. Rusho, and P.T. Reilly.

I am more personally indebted to Mrs. Virginia Jennings, now retired, of the Southwestern Collections, New Mexico State Library, and to Mrs. Petrita Lara of the same staff; to Miss Ruth Rambo and Mrs. Kitty Shishkin (both now retired) of the Museum of New Mexico Library. My appreciation, also, to those various people who helped me look for information at the Anthropological Library of the Laboratory of Anthropology, a division of the Museum of New Mexico.

I thank my daughter, Larwin Michele Measeles-Allen, for additional material on Jim Emmett and Buffalo Bill from the files of the *Coconino Sun;* my friend and neighbor, Mrs. Jan Caldwell McGarrity Saunders, who read the manuscript and was of much assistance with the diacritical markings of the Spanish names; and my special thanks to Marjorie and "Mr. Jack" Lambert (Mr. and Mrs. E.V. Lambert), who read the manuscript with love for well-remembered places and affection for me. Also, Miss Octavia Fellin, formerly of the Gallup Public Library, who forgave long overdue books or picked them up from the post office when trips "off reservation" were too infrequent.

I have tried, in the endnotes, to give credit to all those people whose works I have read, enjoyed, and used. If there are mistakes, I have not erred in intent. For me, this volume has been a long and pleasant experience. I am especially grateful to Dr. C. Gregory Crampton who set me to putting it all together when I read his words, "Many works about the Colorado River refer to Lee's Ferry incidentally but there is relatively little material dealing with it directly."*

*Crampton, C. Gregory, "Historical Sites in Glen Canyon Mouth of San Juan River to Lee's Ferry," University of Utah, Department of Anthropology, *Anthropological Papers* Number 46 (Glen Canyon Series Number 12), June 1960, University of Utah Press, Salt Lake City, p. 97.

Utah Historical Quarterly, Volume XXXVII (37), No. 2, Spring 1969, p. 284.

Regarding the Photographs

My special thanks to the following people for their assistance in locating the photographs that illustrate this book. Without their help, my task would have been far more difficult, if not impossible.

Mrs. Jan Thornton, Special Collections Division, Northern Arizona University Libraries

Ms. Karen Brantley, Park Curator, National Park Service, Grand Canyon, Arizona

Mrs. Barbara J. Bush, Photo Archivist, Arizona Historical Society

Ms. Kathleen F. Leary, Audiovisual Archivist, The Ohio Historical Society

Ms. Sallie Wagner, who graciously volunteers her time for the State Records Center and Archives, State of New Mexico

Mr. Timothy Neville, Photo Archives, Utah State Historical Society

Mr. R.I. Frost, Curator, Buffalo Bill Museum, Buffalo Bill Historical Center

Ms. Evelyn Myers, Photo Archives, United States Department of the Interior, Bureau of Reclamation, Denver

Ms. Phyllis Dennis, Photo Library, United States Department of the Interior, Geological Survey, Denver

Ms. Carol Downey, Department of Library, Archives and Public Records, State of Arizona

Ms. Louise M. Hinchliffe, Library Technician, National Park Service, Grand Canyon, Arizona

Mr. Ron Kinsey, Photographic Archives, Southwest Museum, Los Angeles, California.

To Mr. Walter S. Kahn, Santa Fe, businessman and automobile antiquarian, my appreciation for his time and effort in identifying the automobiles in some of the photographs. To Mr. Emery Lehnert (grandson of the late Emery Kolb, Grand Canyon photographer), my appreciation for the use of the photographs from the Kolb Collection deposited with the Special Collections of the Northern Arizona University Library. And to Ms. Joan Nevills Staveley my thanks for photocopying for me her personal copy of the book by Genevieve and Bernard de Colmont and Antoine de Seynes concerning their trip from Green River, Wyoming, to Lee's Ferry in 1938. I am most grateful for her thoughtfulness.

The quotations from *A Mormon Chronicle, The Diaries of John D. Lee, 1848-1876, Volume II,* edited and annotated by Robert Glass Cleland and Juanita Brooks, are reprinted here with the kind permission of the Henry E. Huntington Library.

Also, through the courtesy of the publishers my appreciation for kindly allowing quotations from the foll·wing books:

McNitt, Frank, *The Indian Traders,* copyright 1962, by the University of Oklahoma Press.

Brooks, Juanita, *The Mountain Meadows Massacre,* copyright 1950 by the Board of Trustees of the Leland Stanford Junior University. Assigned 1962 to the University of Oklahoma Press.

Russell, Donald Bert, *The Lives and Legends of Buffalo Bill,* copyright 1960, by the University of Oklahoma Press.

Stanton, Robert Brewster, *Down the Colorado,* edited and with an introduction by Dwight L. Smith, copyright 1965, by the University of Oklahoma Press.

Stegner, Wallace, editor, *This is Dinosaur: Echo Park Country and Its Magic Rivers,* "Fast Water" by Otis Marston, copyright 1955, by Alfred A. Knopf, Inc.

Staveley, Gaylord, *Broken Waters Sing, Rediscovering Two Great Rivers of the West,* copyright 1971, Little, Brown and Company in association with *Sports Illustrated Magazine.*

Burke, John, *Buffalo Bill, The Nobelest Whiteskin,* copyright 1973, by McIntosh & Otis, Inc.

Contents

The Name

"The name was officially declared to be Lees Ferry (no apostrophe) in the Sixth Report of the United States Geographic Board (Government Printing Office, 1933).*

And it is so, on many maps it is listed as Lees Ferry, and many people prefer it. Others write it Lee's Ferry, and it appears that way on some maps. Because his has always been the pervading presence, no matter how many other people touched it, I think of the crossing with the possessive and have used it in this account.

*Rusho, W.L. "Living History at Lees Ferry," *Journal of the West*, Volume VII, No. 1, January 1968; footnote, p. 74.

John Doyle Lee. According to the notes of the Arizona Historical Society, the original of this photograph was owned by his daughter Amorah Smithson. (See page 9) It is believed to have been made in 1875 when Lee was 63 years old.—*Courtesy Arizona Historical Society.*

1.

Heritage of the River

A tired, wary old man rode south from the settlements of Utah toward America's last great wedge of unknown country, seeking a refuge from the law. Spare, lean of limb, he sat easily in the saddle; only his eyes were alert, watchful for known landmarks, for unknown travelers who might prove foe. His destination was a crossing thereafter through history to bear his name. Even in his own time he was a controversial figure, a man given to dreams, followed by the realities of a massacre whose retold tales would not die. Had John Doyle Lee lived in another age he might have become a benevolent patriarch or even a prophet, but he was born to a different time. Kindly, yet retaliatory by nature, staunch, but made fanatical by the remembered terrors of Mormon experiences in Missouri and Illinois, he was cast up into history as the perpetrator of one of the West's most cruel and unwarranted tragedies, that of Mountain Meadows.[1]

The place to which he rode that raw, sunless November day in 1871 was a crossing of the Colorado, a river known and yet unknown, a river which was then merely a mosaic of time and history.

As early as 1531 the Spaniards heard from the Indians vague references of a large river to the north. Cortés, the once proud conqueror of Montezuma, pawned the jewels of his wife to outfit ships to seek it.[2] But his chosen captain did not find the river, he merely saw the tidal bore and surmised it was there to the north, surging southward to empty into the Southern Sea. Disillusioned, Cortés sailed home to Spain, his favor with the courts now as lost as his Aztec empire. But Spain still had a wondrous share of great adventurers; and where one failed another with a new plan, a different dream, came to stand in the steps of the vanquished.

So it was with the setting of Cortés' eminence, the bright star of Coronado began to rise.[3] Sustained by stories of the fabled seven cities of Cíbola, Coronado left Culiacán, Mexico, in April of 1540 in search of a greater wealth than the Aztecs had to give: cities paved with gold, houses set with the jewels of a pagan empire. Successful in his march north, quartered in the old pueblo of Hawikuh[4], Coronado dispatched Lieutenant Cárdenas[5] with twelve companions to search for the river which came at last to the Sea of Cortés.[6] With Indians to guide them, they stood on the rim of Grand Canyon in the autumn of 1540, the first white men ever to see it. The place where they saw the magnificence of the Colorado is a matter of conjecture, but it is a matter of record that they gazed in wonderment upon it, scarcely believing the words of their Indian guides as to the width of the river below. Three members of the company tried to descend to the canyon floor but could go only a third of the way. They declared the Indians spoke truthfully and assured those who remained on the rim that the rocks which looked to be no taller than a man were in reality "bigger than the great tower of Seville."[7] The tower to which they referred was the Giralda, bell tower of the Cathedral. Thus for the first time the Grand Canyon was contrasted with something familiar, made known, etched in the minds of travelers to be carried as a tale of wonder to others.

Cárdenas did not name the canyon. Befitting his military command, he returned to Coronado's camp and reported the discovery. But the mission of Coronado was merely to seek gold, and his chronicler only noted the adventure and the expedition marched on. Many years passed before anyone was to follow in Cárdenas' wake. Again only the Indians knew of the river and the wonders of its life, places where the beaver were plentiful and the deer came to water and hide in the side canyons. And so for many years the land was as it always was, the river flowed and watered the sustenance of Indian peoples who blessed it in dances that expressed its spirit.

But then an impetus greater than gold activated the Spanish Empire. It became the province of the clergy, and there developed a religious zeal rarely equaled in history, excepting the time of the Crusades. With the coming of the clergy, the black-robed and the brown, the Southwest began to know names other than those of conquerer and colonizer. Faithful, browned men in the frocks of the Franciscan and Jesuit orders established missions, and in seeking new souls for God they looked also for new pathways that might lead from one far-away mission to another.

Two priests whose adventures are often associated with the Colorado are Fray Francisco Thomás Garcés[8] and Fray Silvestre Velez de Escalante.[9] Fray Garcés is considered to be the first white man to have reached the Grand Canyon from the west, about which he was moved to write, "I am astonished at the roughness of this country and at the barrier which nature has fixed therein."[10] The other also kept a detailed journal, and because of it his name is forever associated with the exploration of the great river of the West. He was Escalante, who with Fray Dominguez, on a trek to find a northern mission road to Monterey of California, found a niche in Southwestern history. Forced by winter's weather and scarcity of foodstuff to forsake their initial plan, they now found they must effect a crossing of the Colorado. Of all our rivers this one has been the most miserly in ceding man places to cross its waters. Where the party could reach the river they could not ford. At the place later to be called Lee's Ferry, they made an attempt but were unsuccessful.

Hungry, near exhaustion, they eventually found a likely ford. With their hatchets they cut a few steps into the rock making a way for their horses to descend. With thongs they lowered their baggage, saddles, and packs from the bluffs above and then carefully navigated the way themselves. This became known as *El Vado de los Padres*, the Crossing of the Fathers.[11] It is called by other names—*El Vado*, Ute Crossing, Ute Ford—but people seem to prefer its more romantic name, the Crossing of the Fathers, a tribute to bold, knowledgeable, and adventurous men who in having great love of God, had also great confidence in themselves. This ford is thirty-five miles above the crossing where old John D. Lee tied his horse to the sand willows that November day in 1871, looked out over the land, and called it good. It was here, where the river Paria[12] flowed to meet the Colorado, that he would spend his waning days of freedom, do his last bit for his church, and meet travelers of the unknown wedge of the West. To the end of his days he would call this place home, would seek news of it during his long prison confinement, and would yearn for it as for no other. Here too, at the crossing, Lee would come into contact with travelers, outsiders who carried his name to the world of newspapers in the faraway East. Not all of them were sympathetic to his cause, but the diaries and published reports of these men—writers, historians, photographers, conquerers of the Colorado—reflect from him a generous hospitality and rugged independence.

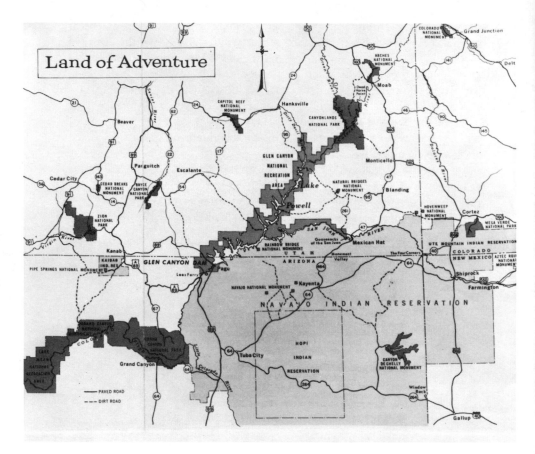

Land of Adventure

Many of the roads shown here as being dirt have, since the issuance of this map, been paved. It is best to check with the nearest National Park, National Monument or Trading Post for current road information. The map is included here because the entire area is truly, as advertised, A LAND OF ADVENTURE.

Lee's Ferry, purchased from the Page Land and Cattle Company on June 11, 1974, became on that date, a part of the Glen Canyon National Recreational Area.

The Ranch, the Ranch House, the Fort and the Post Office are all now listed on the Register of National Historic Places.

The map is printed here courtesy of the United States Department of the Interior, Bureau of Reclamation.

2.

Eye of the Storm and the Outward Edge

The Paria was a quiet place pinned down into nothingness by the receding walls of Glen Canyon and the yawing, narrow gray mouth of Marble. To this day it is a place of magnificence where the chasm of the Grand Canyon truly begins. Though Lee had a responsive spirit, he had little time to gaze upon the beauty created by the river. On this first trip he had, with great difficulty, brought some of his cattle through; now he returned to the settlements for two of his wives and their families. Those to come were Rachel Andora,[13] Lee's sixth wife and sister to Aggatha,[14] his first, and Emma Batchelor,[15] an English girl who had become Lee's seventeenth wife.

Christmas 1871 found them all together at the Paria. Under a temporary shelter they celebrated the Yuletide. Perhaps it was an old-time celebration with a molasses pull, dried fruit brought from the Mormon Dixie country, and parched Indian corn. It somehow speaks eloquently for Lee that here, driven from the economic advantages he had made for himself, burdened as all men are with human ambition, here where he must in old age begin life anew, he could speak with Rachel Andora, Emma, and his children of the wonder and blessing of his faith, and of the fervor with which he held the leaders of his church. His belief in the Mormon religion had caused him sacrifice and privation, but he lived still in its pervading spirit.

It was Emma who, in looking over the countryside, called it a lonely dell. It had a lyrical sound and appealed to Lee, so he adopted it as the name of their new location.

There was not much time for holidaying, as their immediate attention was affixed to the building of shelters for themselves and the livestock which would help sustain them. Rock and flagstone were plenteous and by January 12 they had finished two houses and commenced a stone corral. Emma, heavy with child at the time of their migration, was especially pleased to be among house comforts again. On the seventeenth of January she was delivered of a daughter and named her Francis Dell after the place they now called home. To commemorate the occasion, Lee wrote in his diary, "We Butchered a fine Beef."[16]

Both Rachel and Emma evoke the qualities of pioneer women—dutiful wives, thoughtful mothers who were serene under duress, hospitable to strangers, and courageous in the face of fear. Both had also the additional quality of

Colorado River near Lee's Ferry Bridge, ca. 1927—*Courtesy Special Collections Division, Northern Arizona University Library*

steadfastness in adversity. Travelers report Emma young and comely, friendly and outgoing. She was to remain at the Paria and become a part of its legend. Older and more sedate, faithful to the last, it was Rachel who shared the final haunted years of Lee, who bore the burden and the pleasure of prison companionship when friend and foe alike deserted. She did not remain long on the Paria but repaired to a new ranch that Lee secured at Jacob's Pools.[17]

At dawn on January 19, the household was aroused by a band of Navajos wanting to cross the river. To accommodate them, Lee, Rachel Andora, and two of the larger boys unearthed an old flat-bottomed boat which had been used in previous crossings, recaulked it, and by midday they were ferrying the Indians and their animals across the water. A determined Rachel steered while Lee poled. It was not a gratis crossing; the Navajos traded their way with blankets. Thus the ferry service began.

The Mormons had long known ferrying as a lucrative enterprise. They remembered well the service established by them at the crossing of the Platte near Casper, Wyoming, in 1847, when they left winter quarters for western regions. There the river was swollen from heavy rains and what should have been a ford demanded a ferry. Gentile wagons of westbound emigrant trains were tailgate and hub-to-hub waiting for the waters to recede. The Mormons took over the ferry rights and ferried the Gentiles across, taking cash if need be, but preferring much needed foodstuffs. It paid well and was a lesson in controlled access they never forgot.

Since 1847 the people called Mormons had been in Utah. They had come to the basin which Jim Bridger[18] called his paradise, to build a New Zion, for to them it was a place of hope. Always a provident people, thrifty and industrious, they had in twenty-four years spread out over the territory, laid out towns and villages, and made farms. They brought water to barren places, knew where the grape would take root, harkened to the beauty of growing things. They sent men to seek the Indian and bring him into the church; along with the tenets of their religion, they sought to teach the Indian better farming methods and how to improve his livestock. The tribes with whom they came in contact considered the Mormons a different people from the Americans, referring to the Americans as the "Mericats." Like Old Gabe* before them, the Mormons now numbered few places unknown in the Great Basin.

With the zeal of a missionary and needful of new lands to colonize, the great organizer Brigham Young,[19] who had led the Mormons to Utah, now sought a southern crossing into Arizona. To this task he set Jacob Hamblin,[20] sometimes called the "Leatherstocking of Utah" or, in benevolence and pride, "Old Jacob." Hamblin was a pioneer, a stalwart in the Mormon Church, a missionary to the Indians. Living in southern Utah he knew the trails, the meandering of the river. He knew some of its mysteries, the terrors it could cause; he knew also its quiet places and always he searched for an outlet to carry his brethren of Utah southward. In seeking his Mormon Road, Hamblin made several crossings at the confluence of the Paria and the Colorado. This was the point where Father Escalante and Father Dominguez and their party had

*See endnote 18

John Doyle Lee and two of his wives, Rachel Andora Woolsey Lee (standing) and Caroline Williams Lee. Rachel Andora was one of the two wives Lee brought to the Paria. Later she went to Jacob's Pools where Lee established another ranch.—*Courtesy Arizona Historical Society*

Left to right are John A. Lee (son of John D. Lee), John D. Lee, Brigg Lee (another son) and Amorah Lee, who was at that time 15 or 16 years old.

Some twenty miles from Lonely Dell, Lee built this brush house close to a water hole known as Jacob's Pools. He went there in 1872 to establish a ranch and lay claim to the watering place. Though it was desolate and barren, Lee writes of putting up a cheese press, working on a road to the corral, laying up the foundation for a milk house and ploughing for a garden. He also had a small herd of cattle here.

In late May of that year they commenced building the above brush shelter with Amorah weaving the willows in and out to form the sides. Trimmed willows and their branches were used for the roof and a wagon cover spread over that. Lee wrote they lined it all around and overhead with Navajo blankets.

On June 2nd, E.O. Beaman and two other men came through taking pictures. The above photograph was the result. Juanita Brooks in her biography of John Doyle Lee states that the picture sold widely. It was enlarged and also made up in duplicate to view through a stereoscope.

This, it should be noted, was a temporary shelter for soon Lee laid out a house with a parlor, two bedrooms and a kitchen. By Christmas of that year, he had up three rooms covered with lumber and had put in some cupboards. He had also run out some 8000 shingles from a shingle mill he had brought to Lonely Dell. These he took to the Pools for the house there.—*Courtesy Arizona Historical Society*

first tried to cross in 1776, later making the crossing by fording *El Vado. El Vado* provided a ford, but the route was traveled by horses with difficulty and offered no possibility for use by wagon trains. The confluence of the Paria and Colorado made a somewhat hazardous crossing, but by 1869 was deemed practicable. Brigham Young sanctioned it, and John D. Lee came south to give it his name.

Whatever else he may have been—pompous, dictatorial, quarrelsome, demanding—Lee was also an indefatigable worker, shrewd and energetic. He was an old pioneer who had already become a man of affluence in the Territory of Utah, Deseret. Ten years previous he had been a man of eminence and considerable property with tracts of land, houses, and farms. But the curse of Mountain Meadows followed him, dogged his steps, snuffed out his property, and doomed his role in the church. Though now excommunicated, Lee considered his endeavor at the Paria a mission for his faith. He had, in private interview, been advised by none other than Brigham Young to find a new life for himself. He knew too of the church's hope to develop a southern route to Arizona. Jacob Hamblin told him of the crossing, of the splendid range where stock would fatten; he was advised there was sufficient pasture along the creeks to keep two hundred head of cattle, that the soil was rich and could be irrigated. President Young sanctioned his going. Lee was to secure as many ranches as he desired; he was also to be given word to "step aside" in event of the approach of quarrelsome parties or officers of the law. And so Lee took up a new life; he became a kind of working partner of Jacob Hamblin, who was to receive an interest in proportion to his contribution.

For the first few months of his stay on the Paria, Lee's diary is filled with words of toil, fatigue, and labor. He put in a dam for irrigation and traded Indian blankets to neighbors in the settlement up the Paria for grape roots, choice shrubs, and seeds. He remarked that packing meal by horseback for forty-five miles over rugged mountains was "A hard way to get Bread."[21] A spring freshet broke the dam; with great effort he built it again. The garden began to thrive; Jacob sent grape cuttings and apple trees and coffee. It was primarily, though, to establish a ferry that Lee had gone to the Paria.

To understand why the southern crossing meant so much, it is necessary to know something of the heritage of those who laid claim to Utah. Isolation was as precious as life to the Mormon people. They loved being among their own, living in the way prescribed by their religious faith and yet they could not remain an island. To that end, however, they fanned out to establish a settlement at every spring, branch, or irrigable creek which could be found. To control the water excluded other settlers, and they had come to the region of Utah to be free from those they feared, disliked, or found intolerable because of persecution suffered at their hands.

In 1850, Utah was made a territory, Brigham Young appointed governor, and the federal government reached out to touch them. Under the territorial organization, friction built upon friction: conflicts of law, of ideologies, of religious beliefs, of philosophies took place. People who for a decade had been involved in nothing more political than building homes, making crops, tending orchards, bearing children, now found themselves in a new foment of bitterness.

Both sides protested innocence—religious zeal and territorial government would not mesh. Suspicion propounded distrust. Mormons were accused, justly or not, of lack of patriotism, of rendering service and support to Brigham Young as their religious, economic, and political authority.

President Buchanan,[22] to quell what he considered unrest, sent an army to Utah in the late spring of 1857. Word of their coming reached the territory in July of that year. This inflamed the populace who felt the Army of the United States marched against their own. Now began the remembering of the injustices suffered years previous in Ohio, Illinois, Missouri; the martyrdom of their leader in a Carthage jail; they recounted to their new converts the horror of the winter crossing of the Mississippi, the closeness of winter quarters, the eviction from homes and farmlands, the shattering murder of children at Haun's Mill.[23] They talked among themselves that they had come a long way to find their peace—too far perhaps. Here they would make a stand, turn and fight and in the words of Samuel Richard, "go it for the Kingdom."[24]

To this end they made ready for war, reorganizing their militia, becoming a militarized state, calling their saints home to be with their own, changing their transportation routings for new converts, storing their grain, seeking hiding places in the ravines and protecting mountains. They were exhorted by church orators and their religious zeal was honed to new heights. Indians, with whom they had dwelt so long in peace, now found their favor curried, for the Mormons were desirous of their efforts to help them "or the United States will kill us both."[25]

With these things in Utah; and in Washington accusations, often unjustified, against their polygamous state, their lack of patriotism, their reliance on church authority, their disdain of federal law leaping to new heights in Congressional chambers; with an army marching to their very door, there now fell a perfidious crime upon the history of a church which until then had only crimes others had committed against it to look upon. It was a blot which eventually claimed the life of John Doyle Lee and closed a page of Mormon history forever.

Throughout all this great political upheaval, wagon trains moved westward through Salt Lake and passed without mishap. But the first to cross southern Utah going to California in that year met total tragedy. It was the well-laden wagon train of the Fancher party of Arkansas and Missouri, driving with them over three hundred head of cattle. It appears the group was somewhat divided, one party being a troublesome lot, boastful that they had helped hasten the Mormon departure from Missouri. One man claimed to wear the pistol used to kill Joseph Smith, founder of The Church of Jesus Christ of Latter-day Saints. Some were surly, demanding, and the Mormons had been told not to sell them so much as a kernel of grain.

The Indians, too, eager to plunder and forgotten perhaps in this political tug of war, were now up in arms clamoring for battle. Nerves frayed. Time, circumstance, and the notion that something had to give, finally gave way. Apparently the "roiled-up" Indians attacked the party first as the wagon train rested themselves and their livestock at the place of verdant grass and running water, the place called Mountain Meadows. Some of the braves were killed in the attack. Angry, sullen, the Indians demanded blood. Mormons were there too, initially to encourage them in their attack and to sanction their robbery of the emigrant's cattle and goods, but there had been those who wanted to do away with this wagon train since it started to wend its way southward. When the Indians could not or would not commit the crime for which they had been called to that place to do, when a young member of the Fancher party had been killed as he rode for help, more Mormons were brought in. Some of the men later claimed they were lured to the place of disaster on an errand of mercy, that they were told to go there to bury the dead. (It must be remembered Utah was at this time a militarized state and the men under military orders, but later they could not or would not agree as to who bore the responsibility for ordering the destruction of the Fancher party.)

For five days the Fancher train was under seige. Indians, joined by the Mormon men from the Iron Military District, hovered over them. John Doyle Lee was a major in this militia. Fifty-four white men were there on the ground at Mountain Meadows. The number of Indians has been variously estimated at three to four hundred. Decoyed by Lee from their stronghold, believing the Mormons their protectors, the Fancher party gave up to them their arms, deserted their wagons, and prepared to march the thirty-five miles to Cedar City.

And then the crime of horror took place. Separated from each other, ambushed by Indians, shot by those they believed to be the ones to save them, it was all over in a short while. What had been an unbelieving, shrieking, bloodletting mass of humanity was suddenly quiet. Some say the white men who had helped commit the deed were as quiet as the dead. It was an appalling scene at Mountain Meadows that warm September day in 1857, cattle milling, dust in clouds, whooping Indians, fallen bodies, many showing the desparate attempt by men to reach the women and young ones—and above all, the strange crying of little children who had been spared the onslaught. Over one hundred and twenty adults and older children were slain. All the property of the emigrant train was taken to Cedar City and later dispensed by the church at auction and delegated to individuals who had contracted debt in the name of the church. Lee helped with this distribution.

The magnitude of the crime chastened the emotions of a people who felt somehow things had gone awry, had been carried too far. The white men there on the meadow made a pact of group fidelity never to speak of the deed to others. But the secret was whispered and the deed known openly. Brigham Young was immediately advised, and he did not turn away from the men who had participated, many of whom had been in the first party with his wagons west. For years people outside the church whispered it was Brigham Young who ordered the slaying. Later research has absolved the president of this burden, though it is a matter of record that he protected with the vast powers at his disposal those who had participated.

Lee was close to Young. In one of the old customs of the church he had been sealed to him as his adopted son. The men who were on the meadow were known to each other, to their neighbors, to their church. They wore a stigma to the end of their days: some moved to distant places, some lived quietly among their neighbors who they knew would not turn them over to an enemy.

The federal government in the person of Judge Cradlebaugh and his military escort sought to bring before the law those known to be responsible.[26] Not one writ of the thirty-six issued could be served. Men vanished in the night, slipped away, were warned as though by the wind. The military expedition west of 1857 came to be known as Buchanan's Blunder. Both sides not only blundered, they blighted the attitude between the people of Utah and their government far away in Washington.

After the Mountain Meadows Massacre, Lee lived in southern Utah for fourteen years before going to the Paria. He lived in an atmosphere of lessening kindliness in others, a gradual shifting of the tragic fate of the Fancher party from group guilt to the shoulders of the man who never denied his participation. New converts could not understand his fanaticism; they shrank from his driving ambition to give his all to his church. Among the old members there were those who envied his shrewd trading, his ability to "get ahead." On this note ended the life in Utah that Lee, coming out of Illinois, had made for himself.

John H. Cradlebaugh, United States Associate Justice for the district of Utah. Due to his relentless pursuit of the Mountain Meadows affair, he became a hated public official there.—*Courtesy Utah State Historical Society*

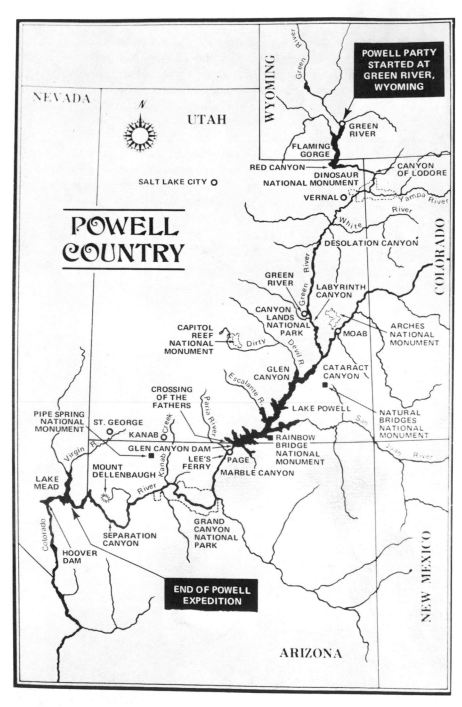

-*Courtesy Utah State Historical Society*

3.

Return to the River

Now to this phase of the river's history came John Wesley Powell.[27] People who do not know of his contribution to it call the canyons of the Colorado by the names he put on his maps. Indeed, the country of the mountain West is richly laden with the names the Powell Party affixed to their new map surveys: Kaibab, mountain lying down; Shinumo, old people; Toroweap, a gully or dry wash; Wonsits, the antelope plain; Paria, elk water, Uinkaret, home of the pines; Paunsagant, home of the beaver; all indicative of a sensitivity to the people who inhabited the "Plateau Province."

Led by his interest in collecting artifacts, flora, and fauna for the Illinois Natural History Society of which he was secretary, Powell in 1867 journeyed westward with several students and interested individuals to the Territory of Colorado. The country held a strange fascination for him: flowers he had not seen; rocks he had not keyed; mountains not yet climbed, but more important, a river not yet conquered: the river which went to the Southern Sea. And so another man came to the Southwest with a dream. His dream he put together with monies from several educational institutions, rations drawn from the United States government, and he welded this together with his own zeal and enthusiasm.

His first descent of the Colorado was a real adventure, full of dramatic incident and to this day offers readers of its history a sense of mystery, intrigue, and tragedy since three of those companions who had come so far left in anger, fear, or frustration just before the expedition completed its mission. The three who left successfully attained the rim of the canyon only to be killed before they reached the southern settlements of Utah by the Shivwit Indians, a Southern Paiute band. Though little scientific knowledge was gained from the initial descent of the river, Powell's expedition captured the public's imagination. He was a romantic figure, a former major of the Union Army who had lost an arm at the Battle of Shiloh. He was also dashing and endowed with courage, determination, ability, and of enviable charm on the lecture circuits.

The trip yielded some general knowledge of directions, currents, and distances, but Powell knew he must have more information before the unknown wedge could become a meaningful part of the country. He had become interested in Indians and their culture and could see a whole new field to be developed in the area of their understanding. Thus he proposed a second expedition and was given a Congressional appropriation of ten thousand dollars to provide

Major John Wesley Powell (1834-1902) in his office in the Adams Building on F Street, N.W., Washington, D.C. Photograph by DeLancey Gill of the Bureau of American Ethnology, Washington, D.C.; date not recorded.—*Courtesy Smithsonian Institution, National Anthropological Archives*

Almon Harris Thompson (Powell's brother-in-law and second in command) of the Second Powell Expedition. He is shown here with his favorite horse "Old Ute." The photograph was made in 1872. Thompson was then thirty three years old.—*Courtesy Arizona Historical Society*

Frederick S. Dellenbaugh in 1872. He was nineteen. The original is from his book, *Romance of the Colorado- Courtesy Arizona Historical Society*

for it. With this new expedition went Professor Almon Harris Thompson,[28] Powell's brother-in-law, who was the chief geographer and a kind of associate with Powell. Also on this trip was Frederick S. Dellenbaugh, a lad of seventeen.[29] To him, this was a glorious adventure and through it he came to love the Colorado, following its storied pathways the remainder of his life, culling legends from others, learning its history from written words and writing, always writing of the Colorado. All of those who have come after him, whether they be real or merely the armchair followers of the river, owe him a debt. The "Grand Old Man of the Colorado" died in 1935, the last survivor of Powell's men who actually made the canyon voyage.

The same fall that Lee came to the Crossing, but a month or so before his arrival, the second Powell Expedition put in at the Paria and cached two of the boats there. Professor Thompson was temporarily in charge of the expedition, Major Powell having left at *El Vado* to go to Salt Lake. The young men were a spirited lot. For them it was camp 86 of a trip that had begun at Green River, Wyoming, on May 22. They were at the Paria eleven days securing packs, making up others to take to the camp at Kanab from where the geologic and geodetic survey work was to be carried on during the winter, spring, and summer months.

It is to the men of the second expedition, no matter how much we admire the dramatic incident of the first, to whom we owe much of our knowledge of the Colorado. During their stay on the Paria they met Jacob Hamblin who was returning from Navajo country with three other Mormon men and nine Navajos. The Indians were going to the Mormon settlements to trade blankets for horses and sheep. The boys did a little trading on their own, Dellenbaugh getting a feather plume for a cap from the Indians and a pair of Hopi moccasins from one of the Mormon men in exchange for a pair of shoes. The evening was a lively one with the Indians and young adventurers doing a round dance to the rhythms of a Navajo chief's drum, which in reality was an upended camp kettle beat upon with a willow root.

In the late summer of 1872 Powell's men returned again to the Paria to prepare for their final assault on the Colorado. Now Lee and his family were at Lonely Dell, and Powell's crew was much impressed by the improvement they had made. There were two or three acres under cultivation in garden stuffs. Grape vines and fruit trees were mere tufts of green, but planted and growing.

The Lees were generous in sharing, and Emma often cooked for the young riverboatmen. Tired of their own camp fare, they were pleased to do farm labor in return for her hospitality. Time hung heavily for them while they awaited the arrival of Major Powell and word to embark. Like all women of her time, Emma knew all about country cooking. She had often cooked for large dinners when Lee entertained the church dignitaries on their traverses through the southern part of Utah. While quick to anger, she was also generous of spirit, fun-loving and outgoing, a person who could enjoy a good joke on herself while turning a neat phrase to josh others. For such a personality the loneliness of the Dell must have been oppressive. Cooking and gossip with Powell's men was one of her few contacts with the outside. Her kitchen was cool in the evening, and the young men were welcome to the things she had—beans and squash, corn, and homemade cheese. They lavished butter on fresh baked bread and spread it over with stewed dried apples. Melons they chose at will from baskets Rachel had learned to weave long ago at the time of Winter Quarters. Occasionally there was also hullcorn and milk, the Mormon Rice, a favorite food of Brigham Young.

In the gathering dusk and by the light of lamps they listened to Lee's yarning. Always something of a mystic, a lover of tales and knowledgeable of men, Lee was also one to interpret dreams—certain qualities of a born story-teller. There was too, on occasion, the delights of homemade beer and Spanish style (roll your own) cigarettes. They celebrated with Lee's family Pioneer Day, July 24, the day commemorating the pioneer's arrival in the valley of Salt Lake. Powell's men called it, perhaps appropriately, "The Anniversary of Mormon Independence."

Major John Wesley Powell in 1891 at Milton, Arizona, where he was a guest of D.M. Riordan. Milton, originally Milltown, was surrounded by the Ayer Lumber Company and wholly owned by it. The Ayer Lumber Company became the Arizona Lumber Company in 1887 when D.M. Riordan purchased the Ayer interest. Milton was a separate community until 1920 when it became a part of the Town of Flagstaff. Riordan, prominent in community affairs, often entertained dignitaries.—*Courtesy Arizona Historical Society*

To repay such kindness they repaired the irrigation ditch, plowed the corn patch, took hoes and worked the garden. Somehow or other Dellenbaugh, now thought of only as the dignified historian of the Colorado, gave the others much cause for laughter by coming up lame while plowing the corn field. It was felt the gentle old plow horse had given him a good kick. Jack Hillers carved teeth for the wood harrow of Jacob Hamblin. The crew got on famously with the Mormon families with whom their lives were meshed for so little a while, and much can be learned of the day-to-day lives of the Mormon pioneers from the now published diaries of the expedition.

At the time they were merely young men out in the wonderful wilderness with a sense of adventure to lead them on. Later they became the old men who were caretakers of the historic West through the books they wrote, the pictures they took, the departments of government they helped to organize. Even the Major got into the cooking act at the Paria, for Lee's diary reports he and the Major "selected some wattermellons & got up a super of vegitables"[31] for Professor Thompson, his wife,[32] and a Professor Demotte,[33] who was a summer volunteer member of Powell's expedition. Lee's diaries mention the crew of Powell's, but it is for Mrs. Thompson, Major Powell's sister, that he had the most admiration. A vibrant personality, loving the outdoors, she accompanied the party on some of its side trips but headquartered at Kanab. Writing his diary, Lee noted, "Mrs. Thompson is a romantic Lady, fond of Mountain scenery. She will Mount a Horse & Scale the mountains with any Mountaineer."[34] Tribute indeed to a gracious lady from an old westerner.

Though Powell never mentioned Lee in any publication and though he acknowledged debt to Hamblin, Lee thought of Powell as being a friend to them. The other party members were less reticient about their observations, and depending on their bent or keenness of mind found him genial, courteous, generous. Perhaps more meaningful to Lee than personal mention in Powell's papers was the Major's adoption of the name Lonely Dell for his maps of the Colorado. Lee was a prideful man and this recognition by Powell indicated acceptance of him, his hospitality and assistance, in a manner which Lee himself approved.

There is a sad and ironical story of one of Powell's men and Lee. The original photographer of the second expedition, E.O. Beaman,[35] left the group shortly after the first section of the journey ended at the Paria. To replace him, Powell hired James Fennemore, a young photographer out of Great Salt Lake.[36] Fennemore was born in England and had come to Utah as a Mormon convert. Accused by other members of the crew as being a bilk and not climbing for views, his contribution to the expedition was nonetheless notable. With Beaman gone and himself ill and unable to go on, Fennemore patiently taught John K. Hillers the science of photography. Hillers went on to become a famed photographer for early scenes of Indians and the Colorado, and he took the first pictures of Zion Canyon. As such his work is invaluable.

Hillers was associated with the Department of Ethnology and with Powell to the end of his life. Throughout his teaching of Hillers, Fennemore grew progressively worse, and it was feared the illness was consumption. Taken to the Lee cabin, he was carefully nursed back to health by Emma and by Lee

John K. Hillers in 1873. He was
thirty. This photograph is from
Dellenbaugh's book, *Romance of
the Colorado,* first published in
1902.
Courtesy Arizona Historical Society

Major John Wesley Powell's boat, "Emma Dean." Emma Dean was the
name of Powell's wife. From F.S. Dellenbaugh in *A Canyon Voyage,* Yale
Western Americana Paperbound, July 1962, page 8: "A wooden arm-chair
was obtained from Field and fastened to the middle deck of our boat by straps,
as a seat for the Major, and to the left side of it—he had no right arm—his rubber
life-preserver was attached." The original photograph was made by John K.
Hillers in 1872. Note: Field was an outfitting place in Green River, Wyoming.
—*Courtesy Arizona Historical Society*

himself. Fennemore always acknowledged his gratitude, saying he could have been treated no more kindly had he been in the house of his own father and mother. When Lee was executed for his part in the Mountain Meadows Massacre, a photographer was there to record the event. It was the young man carefully nurtured back to health there on the Paria who took the final picture of Lee calmly sitting on his coffin, awaiting death. It was also Fennemore to whom Lee gave instructions to send one of the pictures to each of the wives who had been loyal through his long tribulation, Rachel A., Sarah C.[37] and Emma B.. Fennemore himself lived to the age of ninety-two and was the last surviving member of Powell's survey party of the Colorado.

Winter headquarters (1872-73) of the second Powell expedition at Kanab in southern Utah. Here the first map of the Colorado Basin was compiled.— *Courtesy Arizona Historical Society*

This monument commemorated the First and Second Powell Expeditions on the Colorado River. It was dedicated in 1921. Frederick Dellenbaugh and his wife attended the ceremony.

The flag is that of the *Emma Dean*. Emma Dean was the name of Powell's wife and his boat was named for her. Each of the boats had an American flag with the name of the boat embroidered in a field of blue on one side while the stars were on the other. The crew admired these flags greatly, especially since Mrs. Thompson had made them herself. Mrs. Thompson, the Major's sister, was a favorite of the Second Powell Expedition.

In the corner is a copy of Dellenbaugh's book, *A Canyon Voyage,* which was carried on the river by the Kolb brothers on their trip of 1911.—*Courtesy Arizona Historical Society*

Emma Batchelor Lee, wife of John Doyle Lee. She was often mentioned in the diaries and journals of Powell's Second Expedition.—*Courtesy Arizona Historical Society*

4.

The Push South and the Oncoming Tide

In the autumn of 1872 the Mormon hierarchy, fearful of the Grant administration's refusal of statehood and the storms of persecution that might follow in its wake, sought urgently to prepare the crossing of the Paria for a possible emergency exit southward. Most especially they sought to ready the road for an expected exodus of two hundred and fifty families who were to settle along the Little Colorado River. Thus in October of that year there began to arrive at the Dell stout lumber for a ferryboat. Spikes were sent by Jacob Hamblin, and "Uncle Tommy" Smith arrived in December to become "head builder" of the ferry.

Prior to the launching on January 11, 1873, a dinner was spread on the floor of the craft and all twenty-two persons then present at the Dell were invited, including the Indian messenger Tocotaw. The ferry was eight and one-half feet by twenty-six feet, staunch and sturdy, and according to Lee, a light runner. She was christened the "Colorado."* The skiff they used they called the "Pahreah."* Lee wrote in his diary, the "Evening we spent in Social Chat, & singing, then tendered our gratful acknowledgements to the bountiful Giver of all Good, for his Mercy in permitting us to accomplish the desired obJect for the future benefit of the kingdom of God, by Securing the Several watering Places & Stock Ranches, The Ferry with 2 good Boats in complte Running order, togeather with the Farming interes at the Dell."[38]

By April, Lee was doing a thriving business carrying the Mormons southward. On April 23, 1873, he noted he made forty-six dollars. The ferriage charge was "75¢ for each Horse & $3 for each waggon, the Luggage & Men thrown in."[39] He also took foodstuffs for ferriage: sugar, soap, dried fruit, soda, matches, a scythe and snath, anything he could use at the ranch. Later the rate for animals was lowered to fifty cents.

This ferry came to an inglorious end after a life of a bare six months. Near dusk on June 16 a severe storm toppled a tree growing close to the bank against the boat, breaking it loose from its mooring, and it either sank or was crushed by the rapids. It was a sad loss to Lee who found ferrying a means of providing the necessities of life. Lee was a true Mormon, in him there was a gaiety that

*Lee's spelling

even the precariousness of his position could not dispel. Just before the ferry loss he noted the pleasure that could sometimes come in ferry crossings: "finished about noon. My Self & Boys took Dinner with them, then we took the Ferry Boat & 20 Persons took a ride up the river. Had one Lady on Board with us, had Music by the constantina, Dancing & Singing. We had a splendid time."[40]

Miners, lured by the unknown of the Colorado, increasingly crossed at the ferry in their search for the elusive, awesome richness of gold. Lee referred to most of them as "hard cases," meaning for him their reluctance to forget the Mountain Meadows incident. The miners, boisterous and recalcitrant, threatened to turn him over to authorities. They gossiped that the cattle Lee kept at the ferry came from those stolen from the murdered Fancher party and indeed, Lee as Indian Farmer had been delegated the authority to parcel out the goods and cattle taken from the wagon train. However, Lee was never sought on information given to officers of the law by a miner, even though there was a price on his head.

Perhaps in believing good or evil of their fellows, men constantly recognize themselves in each other and refuse to stand judgment and condemn, though facts be known and are abhorrent to them. One miner, Samuel Rogers, was known to remark if the miners did return as they threatened, "you need [not] fear Me. I will come for good."[41] The constancy of being pursued, whether real or imagined, brought to Lee a sense of gnawing, haunting, defeat. He held himself up believing that he would never be betrayed by those whom he held to be the most just, his own religious group. This was his most bitter disappointment.

In spring 1873, there passed a bill in Congress disenfranchising those who would believe in and practice polygamy. In June, Lee left Lonely Dell for Moenave* (near Tuba City, Arizona) believing the United States Army was approaching the ferry with forty wagons and six hundred soldiers. It was believed their purpose was to erect a military fort at the crossing. However, there were not nearly so many soldiers as Lee thought, and they were merely on their way to establish Fort Cameron at Beaver Creek. Lee exchanged his ranch and improvements at Jacob's Pools for a ranch at Moenave, the place of running water. Here, during the summer, he received word that President Brigham Young would be down at the crossing in the fall and a new ferry would be built. And on October 15, 1873, another ferry was launched at the Paria. The boat builders were John L. Blythe and "Uncle Tommy" Smith. The ferry was said to be large enough to accommodate two teams and wagons and their loads. Now the road south was indeed secured.

The boat belonged not to Lee but to the church. This is indicated by a telegram to Lee from Brigham Young and George A. Smith in January 1874: "If you will see that this Ferry is kept up, you are welcome to the use of our Boat. You should charge a suitabl[e] price for your labour. . . . See that your wife Emma gets a proper title to secure the Boat location as probobly the Ferry May be valuable Some day & a support to your Family."[42]

*sometimes: Moeave, pronounced/mownaivi/, from *Arizona Place Names,* by Will C. Barnes.

Lee heeded this advice and made a life for himself with his ranching interest and the ferry. His residence on the Paria, largely because of the pervading spirit he cast over the crossing, has attached to it an element of the romantic. It has been said he worked gold deposits that he discovered near the crossing; that he lived among the Havasupai Indians in Cataract Canyon and brought to them the fruit trees that still grow there—but these are merely legend. His life as a frontiersman was remarkable enough without these embellishments. His laments of extreme poverty during his prison days could not be those of one who held gold in secret, and while he was an "Indian Farmer" there is no published record of his furnishing the Havasupai with cuttings of fruit trees or seeds of vegetables.

On November 7, 1874, while he was in Panguitch, Utah, visiting with one of his families, Lee was arrested for his part in the Mountain Meadows Massacre. Until the summer of 1875 he was held in the Beaver City jail. His first trial was from July 23 to August 25, 1875. It resulted in a divided jury, eight for acquittal, four for conviction. Lee was remanded to prison and sent to the penitentiary in Salt Lake City.

Even while awaiting his second trial, Lee thought of the ferry. In October 1875, he wrote in his diary, "Ralph & John were at work at Pareah with a Team for Molasses, instead of being at the River to assist with the Ferry. I feel Grieved in My heart to think that I am unable to get things in a shape to protect what litle stock & property I have."[43] All through Lee's imprisonment Emma stayed at the ferry. Perhaps some of his stubbornness and endurance had come to be hers, perhaps she had enough of her own. Of her trials at the ferry she wrote him that she "did not feel like faltering & giving up."[44]

The curious visited Lee in Utah prison. Some, through newspaper stories, had come to think of him as the "Great Terror of the West." They found instead an old man called by other prisoners, "Uncle John;" an old man who liked to do farm chores and make the prison garden.

Lee, whose spelling was erratic, could often hover near the poetic in his writing and could always write of those things that mean so much to the researcher, the historian, and those who merely love to read of pioneer days. His diaries remain an exciting account of history in the Kaibab country, and his first-hand writing of prison life in the mid-1870s is an asset to all those interested in sociology. In March 1876, while in prison, he was moved to write in his diary, "Morning pleasant, which strongly remines me of gardening."[45] The curiosity seekers went away strangely moved, and they told him "they did not see any[thing] fearful or Terrific about Me, that they would not be afraid to [meet] Me alone."[46] This was some comfort to him.

In May 1876, he was released on a $15,000 bond with William Hooper as surety. It is said Hooper bought the first of the cattle from those taken from the Fancher emigrant train. Lee's second trial began September 13, 1876, and he was convicted by an all-Mormon jury and condemned to die. There has always hung over his trial an aura of the unreal, of people made ready to talk, to burden one man with the guilt of many. The appeal to the Territorial Supreme Court was unavailing. Like the true pioneer and Westerner he was, Lee chose to be shot instead of hanged. In one of the most bizarre episodes in the history of the West, he was taken back to the place of his accused butchery, the place called Mountain Meadows, to be executed. Calmly sitting on his own coffin, his eyes bound, he raised his hands and placed them over his head so the firing squad could get a clear shot.

He was executed on Friday, March 23, 1877; the following Sunday was Palm Sunday. There were about seventy-five observers. His body was hauled back to Parowan in a wagon. There members of his family received it and buried him with dignity in the cemetery in Panguitch. Thus twenty years later, judgment extracted the death penalty, and for the law, the Mountain Meadows case was closed. It was closed, locked in the hearts and minds of other participants, in the diaries and archive of the church to which Lee gave so much of his life. But it has been reopened since by every reader of the Mountain West, for no matter how the church viewed it, no matter how grisly and unwarranted an affair it may have been, no matter how unfair, uncourageous, or dishonorably the fifty-four white men may have acted toward another of their kind, it has now become an incident of history and is seen in the unforgettable severity of the time and the despairing excess of emotion which gave it birth.

Few are the individuals, groups, or nations whose heritage is unstained. John D. Lee, unlike the others, never denied his presence at the massacre, claiming he had tried to stop it and when he could not that he had wept. And surely his Indian name from thenceforth was Yawgatts, or "Cry-baby."[47] The other participants left him with the moral responsibility for the whole affair, and the old frontiersman paid for it with his life. There would be few who would not acknowledge his was a perfidious crime, but he was not alone. If he could not die with honor, at least he died with courage. Few men can ask more. Of his own part in the massacre he movingly wrote: "My conscience is clear. I have not done anything with an Evil intent. If I have Ered it is in Judgement & not of the Heart."[48]*

With Lee's death, Emma, the strong one, could not manage so great a responsibility alone. Even prior to Lee's execution the church had appointed a man to stay at the ferry and to assist her, and Hamblin himself was at the ferry as a trader during 1874-75. The ferry rights were sold to the church in May 1879, for one hundred cows said to have been contributed to the people of Southern Utah for which they had received tithing credits. When Emma arrived to claim them at Sunset Crossing (on the old route followed by Lieutenant Beale when he crossed the Little Colorado), she received only fourteen head, grudgingly given.

Disappointed, she and her family went to Snowflake, Arizona, where she was married to Franklin H. French, a prospector, whom she had known when he had headquartered above the ferry. French had helped her move her stock and family down to where she was to receive the church herd. After their marriage, they stayed for a while in Snowflake and then in the White Mountain area where they had to take refuge at Fort Apache in the Indian uprising of

*Time being time and history calling again its own, John D. Lee was, in April of 1961, reinstated to full membership in his beloved church, vindicating at last a man who not only made history but who also became its victim (Brooks, Juanita, *The Mountain Meadows Massacre*, University of Oklahoma Press, Norman, 1962, p. 223).

1882. They had been in the White Mountain area for two years and had prospered, but in the uprising all their improvements had been burned. Again they moved, this time to Holbrook and then to Hardy's Station where Emma opened a restaurant. This was the time of railroad expansion and good food was in great demand by railroad workers, cowboys, transients, and travelers to these "western lands." With the restaurant, all the culinary arts she had developed cooking for the big church dinners in her early days in Utah, came to stand her in good stead, for there she had been well-known for her cooking skills; in breads, cakes, and pastries she excelled.

In the late 1880s the family finally settled in Winslow, Arizona, where Emma became the beloved Dr. French, a famous nurse and midwife of that pioneer community. Walter Clement Powell,[49] the Major's nephew who was with the second Colorado expedition, referred to Emma as a "woman of pluck,"[50] and there were references to her courageous attitude with Indians when she was at the ferry that verify the admiration the men of the second expedition had for her. Emma had several children with her at the ferry, for she had been Lee's wife for fourteen years at the time she came there. She was used to hardship and knew the value of courage. Surely no group west exhibited it more than the Handcart Battalion[51] of which she had been a part.

Tradition has it that one night when Lee was away she was awakened by a band of Navajos coming back from the Utah settlements. They talked loudly and angrily of murdering her and the children. Showing more courage than she probably felt, she wakened the young ones and took them out among the Indians, bidding the children make their beds down near the campfire. The Navajos, great admirers of dignity under duress, took this act to heart and on leaving the next morning assured her such a brave one as she would be high in the thoughts of Indian people and would be safe among them forevermore.[52] Thus are the stories told and retold, sharpened, circulated, forgotten in the legends of Lee's life at the ferry.

Emma's removal did not lessen the ferry activity. The year of Lee's execution, the "Paria Road" was considered as a trade route for hauling freight into Arizona. While this never materialized into an official highway, some freight was hauled into Prescott from Utah via the crossing. At that time the distance from the terminus of the Utah Southern Railroad to Prescott was estimated to be 448 miles. A long distance, surely, but not so unbearable as that from Prescott to the nearest railroad which was west of Yuma, a desert journey of over 350 miles.[53]

Warren M. Johnson was the man the church appointed to assist Emma at the ferry when Lee was arrested. For twenty years thereafter he, with his family, as church agent, ran the ferry, and thus it was that a new name came to be associated with river followers. The Johnson family became as much mentioned for their hospitality as Lee had, in his time, been for his. The family has also been commended by some archivists of the river for their work in running the ferry so effectively that during their tenure there were few losses of property and no loss of life.

When the ferry was sold to the Grand Canyon Cattle Company and then to Coconino County, the farm at Lonely Dell was purchased by the sons of

Warren Johnson. After Johnson's release by the church from his work at the ferry, he moved to the southern part of Utah. In a farm tragedy, he fell from a hay load at Fredonia, Utah, and broke his back. He died six years later.

A strange phenomenon occurred at the ferry in January 1878. It was not needed. The Mormon settlers on their way southward found all springs and watering places covered with a blanket of thick ice. It was even necessary to melt snow to water the teams. The river was frozen from one bank to the other. However, above and below the crossing, it was flowing rapidly or as one migrant wrote, it was "open and running." The wagons were pulled over by hand and horses were taken over one at a time. A herd of cattle was crossed by tying the legs of a thrown animal and pulling it over. Mr. Anthony W. Ivins, who was a member of a missionary party a the crossing during this period, wrote that he crossed the river on ice thirty-two times in helping get the wagons across. This was an unusual occurrence and was mentioned in the journals and diaries of that time. [54]

5.

Railways and the River

During the age when the capacity of the country was unknown and the nation was richly endowed with men of vision, a contagion of spirit for new ideas was evident everywhere. Particularly was there great love for the railroads, and it was from this penchant, this potential for moneymaking, that a unique experiment came into being. It had a strange history.

During the late 1800s, S.S. Harper, a prospector-cowpuncher, sought his fortune in the mining districts of the Southwest. He was an astute man, endowed with style and a capacity to see beyond his own campsite. Transcontinental railroad surveys[55] were being made during this time and in his travels, Harper noted that many tough mountain ranges were chosen. Being of a resourceful nature, skilled in a practical way, he came to the idea of building a railroad through the Colorado Canyon, going with the water grade to the Pacific.

In a mining encounter with Denver businessman Frank M. Brown,[56] Harper told him of his idea for the railroad, and Brown, promoter that he was, put these ideas into plans and his many energies into developing a railroad that came to be known as the Denver, Colorado Canyon and Pacific Railway. It was a daring human ambition.

In this day, the project may seem irresponsible, but in that time eminent engineers of Colorado sanctioned the idea, and those to whom Brown talked in the East felt such a railway quite practicable. The then Secretary of State, James G. Blaine[57] of Maine, gave encouragement to it. Brown, in his travels east, made arrangements in New York for financing, dependent on the engineers' favorable report.

With this dream, practical or not, Lee's Ferry became a part of the history of the Denver, Colorado Canyon and Pacific Railway. The company proposed to make a survey starting at Grand Junction, Colorado, following down the Grand to its junction with the Green, then down the Colorado River and through its canyons to the Gulf of California and across to the Bay of San Diego, a distance of 1,200 miles. It was a feasibility study, an effort to see if it really could be done, and if so, to measure its use potential. Some say the sale of coal was a prime motivational force behind this heady enterprise since, at that time, the deposits of Puget Sound had not been developed and California was in need of coal. It was felt that this railway, crossing no mountains and seeking a water level route, could profit from the sale of coal from the Colorado fields.

In the spring of 1889 Robert Brewster Stanton[58] joined the survey party as chief engineer. Stanton's name, superceded by that of Powell, is almost unknown except to river archivists and devotees of the Colorado's history. Yet he was a true chronicler and explorer of the River Colorado. He was a skilled engineer and a fine historian. For many years he wrote and revised his manuscript:

The River and the Canyon
The Colorado River of the West
and the
Exploration, Navigation and Survey of its Canyons
From the Standpoint of an Engineer

Though his official capacity as chief engineer was short-lived, he was to be associated with the river as engineer, mining enthusiast, author, and promoter through much of this life.

Excellent businessman though he was, Frank Brown was no great planner: the boats he had purchased were of thin planking, the provisions had not been well thought out, no life preservers had been provided, and no true boatman of the river had been hired. However, even under these circumstances the crew began their descent of Green River on May 25, 1889, and after tremendous difficulties in Cataract Canyon the survey was carried as far as the mouth of the Paria. By July 2 they were at Lee's Ferry. No supplies had been brought in, so President Brown left by horseback for Kanab, some ninety miles distant, to get further provisions for the journey.

While Stanton mentions the place and comments on the luxury of the edibles they found there, it is to Franklin A. Nims,[59] photographer of the expedition, that we are indebted for details of their stay. They arrived at Lee's Ferry at five o'clock in the afternoon, and the only thing in the grub box was some flour, coffee, and tea. Nims said the place looked like an "Oasis to us. Ripe Apricots, etc."[60] The ferry was then occupied by Warren M. Johnson. He was postmaster, had a store with a small supply of staples and operated the ferry. He and his family provided for this survey party, who moved into the old stone fort there, as Lee had for Powell. They were plied with "green corn, cucumbers, chickens, buttermilk, sweet milk, turnips, sorghum, etc."[61]

Nims noted, "Mr. Johnson . . . has two families and several children in each; mostly girls. One family lives at the Ferry and the other about a mile up the valley."[62] More importantly he wrote, "This seems to be the highway between Utah and New Mexico."[63] Relative to the food he remarked, "Johnson has a fine large garden here and quite a farm by the house up in the valley, and a lot of fruit trees and bushes."[64] And rather poetically, he put down in his notebook, "The Pariah Creek comes winding down this lovely and fertile valley and empties into the Colorado by the old stone Fort."[65]

To celebrate the Fourth of July, the cooks prepared an elaborate dinner. It caused him to comment: "Some layout; will we survive?"[66] The dinner was indeed "a layout" and included:

> Chicken and lamb broth, salmon, roast beef, chicken and lamb, potatoes, squash, string beans, peas, tomatoes, new onions, cucumbers, radishes, lettuce, rice pudding, apple, cherry, custard pies, pinion and hazel nuts, walnuts, coffee, chocolate, sweet milk, buttermilk, white and corn bread, strawberries, apricots, apples, cherries and plums, soda biscuit and oyster crackers, cottage and Utah cheese, cigars, cigarets and pipe tobacco.[67]

From Dwight L. Smith's notes to Nims' diary, the meal also included "potato soup, mint sauce for the lamb, pickles and fruit salad."[68] After the famine of the preceding days before Lee's Ferry, it was indeed a grand dinner.

For both Nims and Stanton it was the first of other holidays to be spent at Lee's Ferry. On July 8, President Brown returned from Kanab, and on the ninth the party departed and camped that night near Soap Creek Rapid. It was on the next day that Brown lost his life in the lower half of the rapid. The loss of their leader was a sorrowful one, particularly so since, though they walked forlornly down the river for miles below, they could not find his body to give it a decent and honored burial.

The leadership of the party passed to Stanton, and however saddened they might be, the next morning the survey party embarked on the river again. As though this one loss was not terror enough, on July 15 two more members of the party were lost. With insufficient men to portage, staggered emotionally by the loss of three men within two weeks, the remaining crew went out of the canyon on July 18 following the path of ancient cliff dwellers. They came to a cowcamp outpost and from there, in the Western hospitality of the day, were escorted to the settlements from whence they made their way to Denver.

Despite the privation, the turbulent time in the canyon, the intense labor involved, despite the losses, Stanton, on reaching Denver, immediately began to plan a return expedition. With backing, renewed funds were raised to outfit the return to the river. Nims, the photographer, was a returnee; one of two. Having left in July they were, by December 10, on the river once more. By Christmas they were at the Ferry again, having arrived on Christmas Eve, riding a high head wind that blew about sixty miles an hour, with waves a full three feet high breaking over the boats.

Knowing they would be in the canyon on this holiday, Stanton had cached in the bottom of one of the boats some treats for this occasion. Christmas was a beautiful day. The cooks outdid themselves in making a splendid dinner. There were flowers from Lonely Dell on the dinner table, which was set in the open air in front of the old Stone Fort.

The menu was as follows:

MENU
Colorado River Survey Christmas Dinner, 1889
SOUPS
Oxtail, Tomato, Chicken
FISH
Colorado River Salmon

ROAST
Turkey, Beef, Ox Heart
ENTREES
Braised Chicken, Game Pie
VEGETABLES
Mashed Potatoes, Stewed Onions, Tomatoes, Rice
Potato Salad
Wheat, Corn and Graham Bread
Tea, Coffee, Chocolate, Milk
DESSERT
Plum pudding, Hard Sauce, Mince and Apple Pie
Apple and Cherry Sauce
Bents Crackers and Utah Cheese
Arizona Apples, fresh Peaches and Pears,
Raisins and Nuts (all grown at Lee's Ferry)
Havana Cigars, Turkish Cigarettes[69]

Stanton Survey Party of 1889-90. Christmas Dinner, 1889. The table is in front of Lee's Ferry Fort. Note flowers on the table.—*Courtesy Utah State Historical Society*

In addition to the fruits, the beef and milk also came from the Johnson Ranch.

Al Huntington, a California "49er," and Mr. and Mrs. Johnson took dinner with them. Franklin Nims made some pictures of the occasion. Perhaps as a result of all the cooking activity for so magnificent a dinner, Nims made a note on December 26, "Both cooks are sick."[70] He also, on that day, made a negative of several men in the party, "in case of accidents below."[71]

Taking a negative of some of the men in the party "in case of accidents" may have also been prophetic for on New Year's Day while striving "to put some life in the picture"[72] as Stanton said, Nims climbed some distance up a cliff to set up his camera and slipped, turned over in his descent, and fell a distance of twenty-two feet, landing on his head and shoulders on the hard sand. Having hit a ledge as he fell, it was found that he had a broken bone in his right leg and a "smashed foot."[73] Being supplied with medicine and bandages, they set his leg to rights using a rubber boot for a crude splint for his broken ankle. They were concerned for internal injuries, for Nims bled fitfully from the mouth.

In what became a somewhat heroic legend of the party, the injured and uncomfortable Nims was strapped on a stretcher made of two oars and some canvas and taken some miles downriver through swift water where, from his notes of the summer previous, Stanton knew of a side canyon to the north, very rugged, for carrying an injured man out to the top. Eight men took turns; and luckily, poor Nims was unconscious most of the time. The crew walked, carrying Nims; slid the stretcher along rock benches, crawling on their hands and knees while others guided the stretcher with ropes. Thus pulling and pushing Nims, hoisting and swinging the stretcher, he was finally pulled from the canyon, the river ledge from which he had fallen some seventeen or eighteen hundred feet below. After a trying night, the wagon which Stanton had gone ahead for, arrived in the afternoon, driven by W.M. Johnson.

One of those who carried Nims to the top was Langdon Gibson, brother of the illustrator Charles Dana Gibson, creator of the Gibson Girl. He is, however, known to the less fashion conscious, not as a brother of the exponent of America's beauties at the turn of the century, but as an ornithologist on the first expedition of Commander Peary to the Arctic regions in 1891-92.

Nims, after his ordeal, awoke on the cookhouse floor of the Johnson family on January 12, having been unconscious most of the time since he was brought there.

The expedition had been forced by a restricted budget to make instrumental surveys at all the difficult points below Lee's Ferry and to reinforce their findings with "complete notes and a continuous photographic panorama of the whole route for the preliminary report."[74] So here was the second expedition not funded for a survey and without a photographer.

Nim's work fell to Stanton, whose experience in photography had until that time been nil, but through necessity he made over 1,200 exposures before he knew how the first had turned out. Stanton estimated that of sixteen hundred negatives he took, a "full ninety per cent were clear, well timed pictures."[75] To his credit he noted, "This was not skill—it was accident, but the kind of accident that is invention, which owes its birth to that troublesome matron so often found wandering in the wilds of the west—commonly called necessity."[76]

Rowing, riding rapids, portaging, rebuilding, packing, repacking, unpacking, rained on, climbing, burnt by the sun, observing flowers and birds and canyon walls, they traversed the way—through Grand Canyon itself, through Kanab canyon, from Grand Wash to the Gulf where they cleared the Custom House at Yuma and entered the Republic of Mexico, and on April 26, 1890, they reached tidewater.

The railroad they surveyed never became a reality; possibly the depression of 1890 was a contributing cause. Stanton himself paid for a large part of the second expedition. By his own accounting he made up a deficit of $12,500. The old cowpuncher-prospector with the original dream helped him even at the end with a donation of $1,500, and Stanton acknowledged his sincere thanks and gratitude.

To Stanton, however, the survey party proved "the line as proposed is neither impossible or impracticable, and as compared with some other transcontinental railroads, could be built for a reasonable cost. From an operating standpoint, it would have many advantages in grades, distance and permanency of its roadbed, and through the driest section of the western country, have an unlimited supply of water, and it would be possible to operate 1,000 miles of its line, yes, the whole of it, by electricity generated by the power of the river tumbling down beside its tracts."[77]

Though the Denver, Colorado Canyon and Pacific Railroad venture died, Stanton's achievement through the Colorado canyons was a triumph. Much later he became a sought after civil and mining engineer in the far-away parts of the world—Cuba, Sumatra, and Canada. But he was not yet finished with the river; he still had a role to play, and there would be other times when he would be a part of Lee's Ferry.

6.

Gold and the River

Gold on the Colorado had long encompassed legend, promise, and fact. The second expedition of Major Powell is sometimes given the dubious honor of having first brought it to the attention of the area. Jacob Hamblin, Captain Pardyn Dodds,[78] and two companions, both prospectors, George Riley and John Bonnemort, had brought supplies to the expedition at the Crossing of the Fathers in 1871, and on that venture found gold in small quantities along the tributaries of the Colorado. Word of their find spread.

Men who loved adventure and the idea of striking it rich had long felt the lure of the area. The killing of Merrick-Mitchell[79] in Monument Valley and the feeling that a magnificent silver strike had precipitated their murder caused many to seek new gravels to pan, new locations for their tents and camp pots. By word of mouth, through newspaper weeklies, the call was carried; and men began to come into the river tributaries of the Colorado for yet another reason.

Cass Hite was one of the better known of these. He had been one of the searchers for the Merrick-Mitchell mine and in his wanderings became friendly with a Navajo Chief, Hoskininni, and legend has it he told Hite where gold could be found on the Colorado. In the early 1880s, Cass Hite came to what was known as Dandy Crossing[80] and discovered gold in the gravels there. The discovery of gold in the San Juans in the 1890s also led to a great infiltration of miners and prospectors into the Colorado River region.

In the *Beaver Utonian* of January 13, 1893, Hite wrote that the great canyons of the lower San Juan and the Colorado had performed the function of mighty sluice boxes; that the fine gold and the richest of the black sands, owing to their gravity, had dragged along behind all the other matter coming to rest, whenever they had a chance. These deposits varied in size and were, in some instances, very rich. From the San Juan canyons Hite wrote with great honesty, "it is the easiest bars or deposits we are always after."[81] Dandy Crossing later became Hite. In time it became a supply station and a post office for the miners along the river. The mail was brought in from Hanksville on horseback. Hite, who was certainly an eccentric and often called a hermit, lived there until 1898 when he moved downstream to Tickaboo Creek. There he died in 1912.

In the first survey trip of the Denver, Colorado Canyon & Pacific Railway, Nims wrote on June 19, "Came down to Dandy Crossing in the afternoon.

"Lee's Backbone." This photograph was taken in 1893 prior to construction of the dugway along the cliff.—*Courtesy State Records Center and Archives, Santa Fe, New Mexico, E.R. Fryer Collection*

Saw Hite City, as it is known; there is a post office here, cliff dwellings, and an old fort across the river. Slept on a shake down. Found good beer here. . . . Several very valuable gold placers here across the river in Trachyte Canon. Miners very hospitable. Wrote letters to send out."[82]

Indeed, more important than the railroad was the mining interest developed by the adventuring Stanton. In his survey work in Glen Canyon, Stanton became very interested in the gold mining possibilities of the region. Nims made a note in his diary that on the railroad survey, "President Brown staked out some placers, but doesn't seem inclined to give us a chance to stake any."[83] However, the very next day he writes, "Hislop, Richards, Gibson and myself staked out a placer claim of 80 acres and named it 'The New York State Placer Mine.'"[84] This claim was on the west side of the river and could not have been far from the Ferry, since he remarked on the same day, "Got down to Lee's Ferry by five o'clock."[85]

Robert Brewster Stanton. This photograph was taken at Trachyte Creek, Glen Canyon, 1897.—*Courtesy Utah State Historical Society*

Stanton himself had staked out gold placer claims. Placers were all through the canyon at the time of the railroad survey. On the second expedition Jack Sumner[86] hailed the crew from the shore asking for tobacco. It was a boon to Stanton to meet him, for Sumner had been with Powell on his first voyage and had gone on to tidewater as Powell had not. Sumner was a fascinating personality, known to those about him as the last of the breed of mountain men. He was a good storyteller, had known Jim Bridger and Kit Carson, and had met Frémont. To him also is credited the naming of the tributary at the end of Narrow Canyon, the "Dirty Devil."

In his summary report to the railroad officials, Stanton wrote of gold mining possibilities in the canyon. He wrote, "From Dandy Crossing to Lee's Ferry, a distance of some 150 miles, the gold placer deposits are almost continuous the whole way."[87] He likely had an interest in a Denver firm's ambition to mine gold along the river. This was the Colorado Grand Canyon Mining and Improvement Company's expedition led by a James S. Best. This company made a trip from Green River, Utah, to Lee's Ferry during the late summer months of 1891, but nothing was done about a mining operation.

It remained for Stanton himself to head the most ambitious project known on the river. He had talked to miners on his preceding trips and his was an observing eye. Though his own mining experience was not extensive, he had done some work in that field, and did serve for two years as general manager for an Idaho Territory mine.

In the spring of 1897, he went east to obtain financial backing for placer mining in the canyon and while in Ohio studied coal mining procedures and types of machinery used in their operation to see if any could be adapted for his purpose. That same year he returned to the Colorado River region to make a series of tests to ascertain the gold mining possibilities through installation of dredging equipment. In this enterprise he had enlisted the support of John Ginty, a California banker, W.R. Mills, a railroad official, Julius F. Stone, an Ohio capitalist, and Frank S. Brooks. He and Ginty were in the canyon in December 1897, testing for gold, staking claims in the upper part of the canyon. In his notebook he noted, in honor of Christmas, he "took a half-holiday."[88]

The tests he and Ginty made were evidently satisfying to the investors, for in March of 1898 they formed the Hoskaninni[89] Company. The investors, besides Stone, Mills, and Brooks, were E.C. Morton and R.K. Ramsey. Stanton himself wore a triple crown: vice-president, engineer, and superintendent. Survey crews were dispatched, and by July they were at Lee's Ferry which headquartered a part of their operation. Counting those made by Stanton and Ginty, the Company had 145 placer claims extending from a little above Hite to Lee's Ferry.

Probably early in 1900, the company developed Camp Stone, named for Julius F. Stone, Ohio capitalist. At Camp Stone was located a blacksmith shop, a tent city housing all the accouterments of a mining operation, plus an ice plant. It was at Camp Stone that the flat-bottomed gold dredge was built on ways, and when finished, allowed to slide into the river. The parts for this dredge were shipped from the Bucyrus Company of Milwaukee to Green River, Utah, and then hauled by wagon to the river for assembly. The distance

Julius F. Stone in 1928.
—Courtesy Photo Archives,
Ohio State University

Camp Stone, headquarters for the Hoskaninni mining venture, 1900. The photograph is by Robert B. Stanton and occurs as Figure 24, p. 172 in Glen Canyon Series Number 15 (Anthropological Papers #54), The Hoskaninni Papers—Mining in Glen Canyon—1897-1902.—*Courtesy University of Utah Press, Salt Lake City, Utah*

The gold dredge was completed in 1900 for the Hoskaninni Company in which Julius F. Stone and Robert B. Stanton were investors. This photograph is by Robert B. Stanton and occurs as Figure 31, p. 177 in Glen Canyon Series Number 15 (Anthropological Papers #54), The Hoskaninni Papers—Mining in Glen Canyon—1897-1902.—*Courtesy University of Utah Press, Salt Lake City, Utah*

hauled was over one hundred miles. Thus another feasibility study for Stanton began. If the venture was successful, additional dredges would be ordered and placed at other locations already staked out.

It was a unique operation for the canyon, all others being poor-boy outfits. The gold of Glen Canyon was extremely fine dust, "flour gold." Most all of it occurred in alluvial deposits, only infrequently in the sandbars. Some of these ancient gravel terraces were two hundred or more feet above high watermark.[90] It has been estimated over "a hundred different types of patented gold saving machinery were tried out in Glen Canyon."[91]

Everywhere the water supply was a problem. Because sand in the water wore out the pumps, gasoline and steam engines were not too successful in obtaining water from the river. At some locations waterwheels were used. The most used type of equipment was said to have been the simple carpet-lined sluice box to catch the flour gold. The gold bearing sands and gravel were dug, shoveled, scraped, conveyed by one means or another to the level of water supply and run through the sluice boxes. Most mines were the operations of adventuresome stalwarts, who were sometimes the lonely men who hailed passing boats for a chat or a bit of tobacco. Most of the work was done by the men themselves, though sometimes there was a horse or a mule to assist in the labor.[92]

Naturally, in view of this, the Hoskaninni Company was viewed as an operational overstatement. There were at one time and another as many as four crews working. A large one worked out of Lee's Ferry. Stanton had his eye on extensive development, and always it seems with Lee's Ferry as a central point. He left stores there, meticulously listing supplies, everything from axe handles and caulking cotton to twelve jars of beef extract and two cans of New Orleans molasses.[93] To show roads, his notes list the following:

January 15, 1898
"Roads to Lees Ferry"

L.F. to Tuba	70 miles 75	
Tuba to Flagstaff	100 miles 85	
To Santa Fe ry	170 miles	160
L.F. to House Rock	45 miles	
H.R. to Johnson	31 miles	
J. to Kanab	14 miles	
K. to Panguitch	70 miles	
P. to Circleville	35 miles	
	(40 to Elsinore)	
C. to Marysville [Marysvale]	25 miles	
M. to Belknap	8 miles	
to R.G.W. Ry	228 miles[94]	

Always, to him, the hub was Lee's Ferry.

It was at the ferry, too, that he did a great deal of assessment work. Then the current American Mining Law stated that it was necessary for any company or individual to expend one hundred dollars annually on each claim in improve-

The remains of the gold dredge built at Camp Stone. This is the way it looked, sunk and abandoned, near Lee's Ferry.—*Courtesy of the National Park Service from the Julius Stone Album*

ment and development. Where claims adjoined, the work could be accomplished on one or several, the total being applied to the grand total for all claims. Thus at Lee's Ferry the crew of W.S. King had built a dirt road. It was ten feet wide and "built along the left bank for 1½ miles above the ferry. The road at the ferry and up over 'Lees Backbone', the sharp ridge below the ferry on the left side was improved."[95]

Whatever its proofs for improvements, whatever its dream, the machinery on the dredge was too inefficient to save the flour gold, and though Stanton maintained it was feasible if greater capacity dredges were used, he argued without avail, and on September 27, 1901, the Hoskaninni Company went into receivership. Estimates of expenditures for the company ran from one hundred thousand to three hundred and fifty thousand dollars, though the initial figures are probably closer to the actual amount. Eventually the old Hoskaninni claims reverted to public entry, since there was no effort to keep up the assessment work. Thus Stanton, who knew and loved the river so well, was doomed to failure for a second time.

This was not the last of Lee's Ferry and the Gold Rush, however, for in 1910-11 another company, the American Placer Corporation, was formed in Chicago. This time the gold prospects were in the Chinle formation at the ferry itself and in the area of both sides of Marble Canyon downstream from the Paria.[96] Another imaginative engineer was in charge. His name was Charles H.

Spencer. On the San Juan he had had a mill for crushing Wingate sandstone, which carried low values of gold and silver. But his operation, like the well-financed Hoskaninni Company, was not a commercial success. In the meantime, an engineer, W.H. Bradley, from the interest backing Spencer, discovered that the Chinle formation underlying the Wingate carried better values in gold than the Wingate. "Spencer abandoned his San Juan project transferred operations to Lees Ferry where the Chinle shales are found close to the banks of the Colorado."[97]

The operations center was at Lee's Ferry, and steam boilers were to operate the pumps to provide the water for placering and hydraulicking. For this purpose two coal mines were developed in Tibbet Canyon. Like Stanton's Hoskaninni outfit, this one also built several rock buildings to serve as offices, shops, and quarters for their operation.

It was the American Placer Corporation that assembled the steamboat of the Colorado, the *Charles H. Spencer*. This was in 1911. The parts were brought in from San Francisco, and it was assembled along the right bank of the Colorado at the mouth of Warm Creek. The cost of the boat was $30,000, and it was named for the engineer in charge of the American Placer Corporation's operation at both the Ferry and Warm Creek. It was 92 feet long, had a 25 foot beam, and was driven by a 12 foot stern paddle wheel powered by a steam boiler.[98] The boat was launched in February 1912. It was of this boat that Kolb wrote "on rounding a turn we saw the strange spectacle of fifteen or twenty men at work on the half-constructed hull of a flat-bottomed steamboat, over sixty feet in length. The boat was on the bank quite a distance above the water, with the perpendicular walls of a crooked side canyon rising above it. It was a strange sight, here in this out-of-the-way corner of the world."[99] "The vessel was to be used to carry coal down the river to a dredge that had recently been installed at Lee's Ferry."[100]

Emery and Ellsworth L. Kolb[101] were running the river that year of 1911, having left Green River in September. At the Ferry itself they were met with a cry of "There come the brothers."[102] They were warmly cheered and hosted to a "well-cooked and substantial meal."[103] Some of the Johnson family were there still, postmastering, the mail at that time being brought in "from the south, a cross-country trip of 160 miles, through the Hopi and Navajo Indian Reservations."[104]

Kolb wrote that at Lee's Ferry there were at least six or seven other buildings besides the large stone one that served as a dining room. The buildings were "so arranged that they made a short street, the upper row being built against a cliff of rock and shale, the other row being placed halfway between this row and the river. These buildings were all of rock, of which there was no lack, plastered with adobe or mud."[105]

Kolb also wrote of how the dredge operated. "One feature about the dredge interested us greatly. This was a tube, or sucker, held suspended by a derrick above a float, and operated by compressed gas. This tube was dropped into the sand at the bottom of the river and would eat its way into it, bringing up rocks the size of one's fist, along with the gravel and sand. In a few hours a hole, ten or fifteen feet in depth and ten feet in diameter, would be excavated.

The Charles H. Spencer, photographed at Lee's Ferry sometime in the late fall of 1911.—*Courtesy Northern Arizona University on behalf of the Kolb Collection, Copyright 1977 by Emery Lehnert*

Then the tube was raised, the float was moved and the work started again. The coarse sand and gravel, carried by a stream of water, was returned to the river, after passing over the riffles; the screeing which remained passed over square metal plates—looking like sheets of tin—covered with quicksilver. These plates were cleaned with a rubber window-cleaner, and the entire residue was saved in a heavy metal pot, ready for the chemist."[106]

The coal, mined in Tibbet Canyon and stockpiled, was loaded on the launched *Spencer,* and she made a trial run to Lee's Ferry and back again. But the steamboat, like the dredge, was doomed to failure. It drew too much water at low level, and the unkind story goes she used all the coal she could haul down to make the trip back up. It was a distance of twenty-eight river miles and required two days to make the trip. Though several were made, the operation was considered unsuccessful and the riverboat was tied up at Lee's Ferry.[107]

After this, smaller boats were employed for use and eventually pack trains were resorted to, but they could not supply sufficient coal to keep up the gold mining operation.[108]

The suspension of this Corporation's mining activities in 1912 brought to a close extensive gold mining operations centering around the ferry. The gold fever started by Pardyn Dodds, the horse wrangler of Powell's, and accelerated by the panic of 1893, ended with finality in 1912. Perhaps the men who obtained the most were those who did not seek so much—those who worked the one-man, one-horse operations, who found only a precarious livelihood, but were at one with the canyon.

Other interest were later developed in the environs of the river—copper and petroleum, but those affected Lee's Ferry but little.

On road to Lee's Ferry with mining supplies, 1910.—*Courtesy Northern Arizona Pioneers' Historical Society Collection, Special Collections Division, Northern Arizona University Library, William H. Switzer Collection*

The Ferries

The Ferry, ca. 1920's. Note building on the right.—*Courtesy Department of Library, Archives and Public Records, State of Arizona*

Pulling in freight wagons...Lee's Ferry, no date.—*Courtesy Department of Library, Archives and Public Records, State of Arizona*

Freight wagons...Lee's Ferry, no date.—*Courtesy Department of Library, Archives and Public Records, State of Arizona*

Freight wagons...Lee's Ferry, no date.—*Courtesy Department of Library, Archives and Public Records, State of Arizona*

Lee's Ferry, Arizona, 1922. Jerry Johnson is on shore. The truck on the ferry is a Model T Depot Hack.—*Courtesy Utah State Historical Society*

One of the numerous ferries operated at the crossing.—*Courtesy Special Collections Division, Northern Arizona University Library, Frank Gold Collection*

Ferry crossing the river at Lee's Ferry, Arizona, ca. 1920's. There are conflicting dates as to when the cables were attached to facilitate the crossing. One is 1896; the other is 1898.—*Courtesy Northern Arizona Pioneers' Historical Society Collection, Special Collections Division, Northern Arizona University Library, George Hochderffer Collection*

Ferry, "dockside."—*Courtesy Northern Arizona Pioneers' Historical Society Collection, Special Collections Division, Northern Arizona University Library, P.T. Reilly Collection*

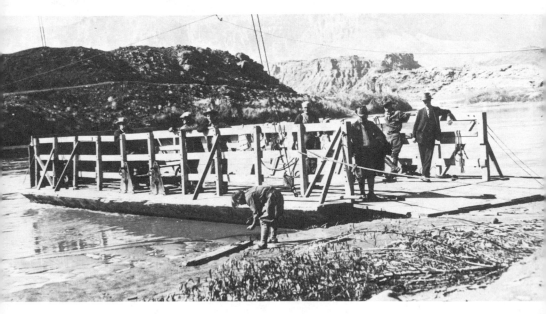

Lee's Ferry.—*Courtesy Utah State Historical Society*

On the Ferry in March of 1921.—*Courtesy National Park Service, Collection of Wilma Hugget*

Crossing at Lee's Ferry, ca. 1924. The man standing by the car is James
Kennedy, Chairman of the Coconino County Board of Supervisors. The car
on the ferry is a Studebaker.—*Courtesy Northern Arizona Pioneers' Historical
Society Collection, Special Collections Division, Northern Arizona University
Library, Frank Gold Collection*

Lee's Ferry, 1925. "The evermoving sand of the Colorado River stalled the ferryboat at Lee's Ferry and caused the passengers to wade." The passengers are "Mr. Stahl, Santa Fe Agent, Mr. Thomas of Flagstaff, School Superintendent, Dr. Mackey 'the horse', Dr. Felix Manning 'horseback'." Information on photograph from George Hochderffer.—*Courtesy Northern Arizona Pioneers' Historical Society Collection, Special Collections Division, Northern Arizona University Library, George Hochderffer Collection*

Governor George W.P. Hunt at Lee's Ferry, ca. 1920's. He was the first Governor of the state of Arizona. From 1912 until 1933 he served seven terms in that capacity.—*Courtesy Northern Arizona Pioneers' Historical Society Collection, Special Collections Division, Northern Arizona University Library*

Part of a large group of men who worked on the dugway, ca. 1898. The man fourth from the left is Samuel Alverius Mechan, contractor for the dugway.— *Courtesy State Records Center and Archives, Santa Fe, New Mexico, E.R. Fryer, Collection*

This photograph shows a view of the Dugway which was built about 1909. It replaced the road favored by the pioneers of the 1870's. That road had been laid out by John D. Lee and climbed alongside of "Lee's Backbone." There is a disparity of eleven years in the two dugway pictures. It is possible the work continued for that length of time. I have used the information on back of the original photographs.—*Courtesy State Records Center and Archives, Santa Fe, New Mexico, E.R. Fryer Collection*

Lee's Ferry, 1921. This group was well prepared...note ropes, canteen, camping equipment. The car is a Studebaker.—*Courtesy National Park Service, Collection of Wilma Hugget*

7.

Welding of the Intermountain West

Thirty-two years after the ferry rights were purchased from Lee's widow the authorities of the church sold them to the Grand Canyon Cattle Company, a group which had its roots in California and grazed its cattle in the famous Kaibab and expanses to the north. A year later the property changed hands again. Coconino County bought it and operated the ferry as a public venture. In 1913 a private company contracted to run the ferry for a specified amount each year. This contract lasted only three years when the county took it over again and ran it as a public property until the highway bridge[109] was completed in 1929.[110] Travelers to the west previous to that year crossed at the Ferry. Open touring cars, the Ford "Tudor," the "Tin Lizzie" with its brass radiator and wooden dashboard, the snappy roadster, the Packard "twin six," and the Pierce "Great Arrow," an occasional Navajo on his pony—they all knew it—a link between north and south; a hot, sultry place in summer; cold, remote, somber in winter; a winding, seemingly endless descent any time.

On July 29, 1927, the contract was let by the Arizona Highway Department for a bridge to cross Marble Canyon downstream from the Ferry. To many, the year 1929 creates still a certain bleakness of heart, but June 14 of that year brought to Arizona and Utah a feat of engineering magic. On that date the Navajo Bridge was dedicated, welding together at last the intermountain country of the West. Six thousand people witnessed the event. Four governors and the head of the Mormon Church were present. It was a two-day celebration. Old-timers who had worked the placer mines of the eighties, whiskered men of the river, cowpunchers, Navajos like bits of color in Pendleton blankets, Mormon people from the settlements, rubbed elbows with officials of railroads, dudes, businessmen from the East, engineers, news cameramen, the curious and the newly courted tourists to Western lands. It was estimated the photographs taken these few days would paper the walls of Grand Canyon itself for a distance of ten miles.

It was a real extravaganza put on by the Arizona Industrial Congress, the Arizona Chamber of Commerce, and the State of Arizona working tirelessly together. They built a little town with a small hotel, erected countless lemonade stands and booths for selling hot dogs, constructed tents for the developing of photographs, put up information booths, and built a "Slippery Gulch" Dance

Touring, Marble Canyon area, March, 1921.—*Courtesy National Park Service, Wilma Hugget Collection*

Lee's Ferry as it was in 1921.—*Courtesy National Park Service, Collection of Wilma Hugget*

Lee's Ferry Bridge under construction, ca. 1927.—*Courtesy Special Collections Division, Northern Arizona University Library*

Lee's Ferry Bridge under construction, ca. 1927.—*Courtesy Special Collections Division, Northern Arizona University Library*

Lee's Ferry Bridge under construction, ca. 1927.—*Courtesy Special Collections Division, Northern Arizona University Library*

Hall which was a popular gathering place. To solve the water problem, a pipe-line was laid five miles to a spring, and the water was piped to a large tank. It was a favored meeting place and crowds of people were there constantly—getting water to drink, to cook with, or to wash in. The small hotel was for the accom-modation of the more honored guests, and the other thousands camped. Ice was plentiful, lemonade in abundance.

Indians danced and gave an exhibition of Indian sports. Two thousand of them had come, along with their superintendent, from the Western Navajo Agency. Perhaps there was among them some who had heard in their own hogans the story of Dellenbaugh and young Walt Powell dancing with the Navajos long ago around the forgotten campfire of the Paria.

It was a wonder—dust-caked people, thousands of them, from all parts of the country, coming to the Paria where there was again something of greatness happening in the West. All of the people, and all of the equipment to build the bridge they were to see dedicated, and all of the supplies hauled in to make the occasion a happy one, had come over a hundred miles through washes and Chinle hills, made like rainbows with lavenders and greens. That day, the way for one hundred miles in the four directions gave out the news, "To Grand Canyon Bridge." In the happy way people were then, eager to be in on the day of jubilation, cars moved across the bridge at night in a never-ending stream—a regular mechanized torchlight parade. An impromptu dance was staged by the Navajos in the middle of the bridge causing a traffic jam. Flags whipped in the breeze, bands played. But it was more than oration and music, more than campers reminiscing around campfires, more than reunions and old time songs—it was the fulfillment of dreams the West had cherished: to open a way, to establish a link, to build a bridge where once only a crossing had been to show America the scenic wonderlands of the Mountain West.

Such a portentous occasion was followed by a lull of years. The hoped-for highway was built, crawling through House Rock Valley to Jacob's Lake. Faster cars and more tourists zoomed over Navajo Bridge pausing to look upon the grandeur of the canyon, but many unknowing of the history made at Lee's Ferry. Then came a bit of notoriety again. In 1935, headlines blazed it as a polygamous stronghold, and indeed the publicity reached such proportions the church took official notice of the scandal. Polygamy had been outlawed by the Mormon hierarchy prior to Utah's admission to the Union. President Wilford Woodruff,[111] under federal pressure and in the best interests of his people, had issued a manifesto against plural marriage, though he did not deny the divine origin of the tenet. Much ado was made by the press, but the incident best remembered is the waggish comment attributed to Governor Hunt of Arizona. He had been making his own inquiry into the affair and after a long, hot trip to the area is said to have remarked, "Hell, if I had to live in this place, I'd want more than one wife myself."

But neither the publicity nor the people's interest stayed on Lee's Ferry for long. It became again only the river, the wind, and the cottonwoods surrounded by the awesome, sometimes savage beauty of a country threaded by the magnifi-cent river. And it was thus for almost twenty-seven years after the dedication of the bridge, a land of great magnitude where the walls of Glen Canyon slipped away; where the Echo and Vermilion Cliffs stood in colorful splendor; where solitude was a way of life; where old stories came to haunt and new legends awaited their creation.

Lee's Ferry Bridge.—*Courtesy Special Collections Division, Northern Arizona University Library*

The Lee's Ferry Bridge

Navajo Bridge Dedication, 1929. In the first line of cars, left to right, note the Pierce Arrow, the Lincoln, a Model A roadster pick-up and the two Chevrolet trucks further right.—*Courtesy Utah State Historical Society, Collection of A.L. Inglesby*

"The formal dedication of the bridge occurred shortly after 1 p.m. Friday in the presence of the governors and other assembled officials in the middle of the structure, where the four state flags and the Star Spangled Banner whipped briskly in the breeze and the spectators loaded the bridge to capacity. Governor Phillips read the brief, formal declaration and cut the ribbon barrier and his charming daughter Miss Elizabeth Phillips cracked a bottle of ginger ale against the rail amid lustly cheers from Salt Lake to Yuma. The ginger ale splattered the delighted spectators and the broken glass went into the bottom of the Marble Gorge."

Quoted from the Santa Fe New Mexican of June 17, 1929.

Governors attending were:
Governor J.C. Phillips of Arizona
Governor F.B. Balzar of Nevada
Governor R.C. Dillon of
    New Mexico and
Governor George M. Dern of
    Utah. Former Governor George
W.P. Hunt of Arizona also
attended.

The panoramic photographs of the bridge at Lee's Ferry, shown above and on the preceeding pages, were made with a special panoramic camera. This camera operates in much the same way as an ordinary camera, with one special difference. The type of lens on a 'pan' camera has a slit aperture, allowing the lens to move horizontally across the film that is held on a curved back plate, thus producing a photograph with a wide field of view. Most panoramas cover an angle of vision between 90-180 degrees. Information courtesy Special Collections Division, Northern Arizona University Library.

Another method of producing a panorama is to take several photos while rotating the entire camera horizontally across the field of view, then fitting or overlapping the photos to produce the desired effect.

The reason panoramas are made is to give the viewer an entire scene that could not otherwise be put on one photograph without moving so far back from the subject that the diminished size would significantly lessen the intended effect.

These photographs of Navajo Bridge were made during the time of the dedication, a two-day event in June, 1929. The photographers were the Kolb Brothers, and the photos are here reproduced through the courtesy of the National Park Service.

Note: Most often, to the people, it was Lee's Ferry and Lee's Ferry Bridge and the photographs they gave to the historical societies and libraries so declare it. I have given the name here as it has been listed on the photographs.

Cars lined up at Navajo Bridge Dedication, 1929.—*Courtesy Utah State Historical Society*

Lee's Ferry Bridge.—*Courtesy Special Collections Division, Northern Arizona University Library*

Pickwick Stage at Lee's Ferry Bridge dedication. A.L. Rogers and O.D. Flake (driving). The names of the cities around the top of the stage read El Paso, San Diego, Los Angeles, San Francisco, Portland, Seattle. The Pickwick Stage later became the Greyhound Bus Company.—*Courtesy Arizona Historical Society*

Giving the Pickwick Stage an assist from the sand at Lee's Ferry Bridge Dedication.—*Courtesy Arizona Historical Society*

George Wharton James with camera and equipment at Grand Canyon.—
Courtesy Southwest Museum, Los Angeles

8.

Adventurers of a Different Order

Waterways have always held strange fascination for man. With only a need to know, he sought their source and marched long distances to where they came at last to the sea. The Colorado is a river in the grand tradition, yet it has remained stubborn and sequestered. But with all its grandiloquence, its appeal to the brave and to the foolhardy, it is not altogether theirs, for it is also a river of dreamers. Therein has been its strength, its wide contrast, its paradox. Each man who has claimed it has done so in accordance with his own dream.

Many men, because of their association with the river, should have their stories known. They were trappers in the tradition of the mountain men; they were writers and lecturers; they were explorers and boatmen; they were photographers and adventurers. Some wrote of their time at the Ferry, some had their stories told by others, and some came and left with no story at all. Of the many, only a few are remembered here.

George Wharton James

Among others who came to Lee's Ferry was the beloved old blanket man of the Southwest, George Wharton James. He had visited the area of the Grand Canyon on trips of varying duration when his book *In and Around the Grand Canyon* was published in 1900. James was a Britisher, having come to the United States when he was twenty-three. For seven years he was a Methodist minister in Nevada and California. Due to problems of health, he came to the Southwest, which he studied and photographed for the rest of his life.

Turned lecturer, he spoke on the Chautauqua circuits and in educational institutions. He also turned to writing. His special interests were in the old missions of California and the Southwestern Indians. Throughout his years, he collected books on the Southwest, and his excellent library was a gift of his widow and stepdaughter to the research library of the Southwest Museum of Los Angeles.

In 1897, Wharton was at Lee's Ferry and like others before him was delightfully surprised by its beauty, admitting that in crossing "the actual presence of the rapids to our right and left, their fierce, angry, deafening chorus, together with the narrow and precipitous walls of the mouth of Marble Canyon close by, made us feel the necessity of having ferrymen with sturdy arms, vigorous lungs, and a thorough knowledge of their business. Arrived on the other side, it was but the work of a few minutes for our horses to pull the wagon through the soft sand, to what seemed to our desert-stricken eyes a perfect paradise. There surrounded by towering walls, glaring back in brilliant reds, crimsons, vermilions, greens, oranges and yellows, was the scene of the arduous labors of the notorious Lee. Large alfalfa fields, almost equally large vineyards and orchards of apples, pears, peaches, plums, cherries, etc., and a vegetable garden stocked with thriving potatoes, squash, beans, tomatoes, melons and everything that one could desire, the whole irrigated with water diverted from the Paria Creek, had taken the place of the sandy waste that Lee originally found."[112]

While at the Ferry he persuaded Nathanial Galloway to take him from Lee's Ferry up Glen Canyon to visit Galloway's placer claims and down Marble Canyon where Galloway was also interested in prospecting. On the lower trip he took a "box of fine grapes and other fruits from the Lee's Ferry orchard."[113]

Nathaniel Galloway and Julius Stone

General Ashley,[114] in 1825, had traveled in his bullboats[115] down to the mouth of the Uinta seeing beaver sign and marking a suitable place for a rendezvous. Denis Julien, working his traps out of Fort Robidoux in that same valley of the Uinta, left his name and the date 1836 on the cliff walls of Cataract Canyon.

But the days of the mountain men and the fur trapper were gone. Jim Bridger and James Clyman, among the most long lived of the lot, had died in 1881; Jedediah Smith, one of the best, had gone, a victim of Comanche lances, fifty years before. Though the day of the rendezvous had long passed, some of the people who had come to the southern part of Utah as prospectors and farmers made an additional livelihood through a sideline of trapping. One such was a Mormon by the name of Nathaniel Galloway. He had worked the Colorado and Green River areas since 1884, and by 1896 had five times been through the canyons of the Upper Green. In the fall of 1895, on a trapping venture, he left Green River and descended the Colorado as far as Lee's Ferry. In fall, 1896, he, his son Than, and a companion William Chesley Richmond went down the Colorado, arriving at Needles, California, in February 1897.

A knowledgeable and practical man, Galloway designed his own boat for canyon travel and developed the stern first technique, which became standard for river runners. There is also Galloway Cave, visited by him in 1894 and named for him, although some now call it Outlaw Cave.

When Stanton was doing assessment work and building roads, Galloway went to work for him for cash monies. It was here he met Julius Stone, a coal company official and capitalist friend and associate of Stanton. Known as a good storyteller, it is likely Galloway had a ready audience in Stone, who was an outdoorsman enthralled by the beauty of his surroundings and the wonder of the beckoning river. They became fast friends. While Stone was visiting the placer operations of the Hoskaninni Company in 1898, Galloway took him through Glen Canyon to Lee's Ferry.

Nathaniel Galloway and Julius F. Stone (wearing glasses). This photograph was made at the time of the Stone Expedition of 1909.—*Courtesy Utah State Historical Society*

Though many had now been on the river with measuring or mining in mind, the time had not yet come to run the river just for pleasure and adventure. It had been twelve years since Stanton had interested Stone in the mining venture of 1897, eleven years since Galloway had taken Stone on a trip through Glen Canyon to Lee's Ferry. All during this intervening time Stone had planned another Colorado River trip, going all the way to tidewater. He had Galloway come east to supervise the building of his boats.

Julius F. Stone during his trip through Glen Canyon in 1938. He was 83 years old.—*Courtesy National Park Service*

On September 12, 1909, Stone and a party of four left Green River, Wyoming, and made a successful run to Needles, California, arriving there November 19, 1909. This was the first river trip planned and executed on such a grand scale just for love of adventure, though photography and exploration of the river was a part of it.

Stone wrote movingly of his time on the Colorado, of his love for it, and his admiration for the men who had come to know it. He had especially high regard for Galloway who, he said, "remembers nearly every turn in the canyon,"[116] and he felt him so equipped to handle a boat on the river that he noted "he is so dextrous that one would not be surprised to see him run a boat on a heavy dew if it were necessary."[117] He remarked that Galloway trapped for beaver in the canyon, shipping the pelts to Chicago from Green River, Utah. Others, trapped in the Colorado Canyon, were made ready for shipment from Needles. They trapped no otter, though they saw some tracks. On October 27, 1909, they camped among the willows of Lee's Ferry. On October 28, "four men came in from Searchlight, Nevada, enroute to Wrights Bar, 25 miles upstream."[118] At that time there was much activity up and down the river due to the American Placer Corporation staking out the countryside around Lee's Ferry.

The resplendence of the nights in the canyon Stone found especially lovely. He wrote of the constellations Venus, the Swan, the Andromeda nebula. He commented on the bobcats and butterflies he saw, on the deer, and on the fish.

For others who said it less well or perhaps said nothing at all, Stone wrote, "Often and long I shall recall the incomparable exhilaration that came just as I felt my boat slide into the troubled waters of the wilder rapids, only to vanish with the breakers at the foot. All other outdoor experience that I have ever known is feeble and flat in comparison."[119] Sadly he wrote, because he had found joy here, "In all probability I shall never be on the River again."[120]

Stone returned to his home in Ohio, Galloway to southern Utah, where he prospected and trapped with varying degrees of success.

Galloway ended his river career at Lee's Ferry in November of 1912, on a last venture with Charles Smith from Green River, Utah. Galloway died in 1913, the year in which his last river partner was "unreported" from a trip through Cataract Canyon. Part of Smith's boat was found in Glen Canyon near Tickaboo Creek.

Zane Grey

Zane Grey, the most well-known writer of the Western novel, came to the land he was to write about so often and so vividly, in the year 1907. He had been to the Grand Canyon in January of the year previous, when he and his wife, Dolly, were on their honeymoon. They were then bound for California and like most tourists of their day, they stayed at El Tovar and took the trip down into the canyon.

In 1907, Grey met Buffalo Jones (J.C. Jones), who was a lecturer at the Campfire Club in New York City. Jones was there in hopes he could raise money to finance his cattalo project. He had been a buffalo hunter in the 1870s, a game warden at Yellowstone, and in more recent years an ardent

Zane Grey with Navajo Indians.—*Courtesy Ohio Historical Society*

Left to right, James Emmett, Buffalo Jones and a Navajo helper . . . note lions in the panniers.—*Courtesy Ohio Historical Society*

THE LAST OF
THE PLAINSMEN
ZANE GREY

Cover-jacket from *The Last of the Plainsmen* by Zane Grey. The book was a biography of J.C. "Buffalo" Jones. It was Jones that Grey came west to visit. Inspired by his western experience, his first novel, *The Heritage of the Desert* was published in 1910.—*Courtesy Ohio Historical Society*

Zane Grey in camp.—*Courtesy Ohio Historical Society*

champion of the buffalo, which was then being threatened with extinction. "He had a small ranch on the rim of the Grand Canyon in Arizona where he was experimenting with the hybridization of buffalo and black Galloway cattle, hoping to produce a breed capable of subsisting on the natural vegetation of the desert and a minimal amount of water."[121] He called his hybrid cattalo. Jones' eastern audience was unbelieving that such a thing could be done, although they responded to his motion pictures of capturing wild animals with a lasso.

One of the few interested was Zane Grey, who proposed to accompany Jones to his ranch, see the operation, and write a book about his work which would, they hoped, interest people in helping to finance his project. Grey paid his own expenses for this trip. He went first to El Tovar, then returned to Flagstaff where he was to meet Jones.

It was while they were waiting for another member of the party, whom Jones hoped to interest, that Grey was introduced by Jones to Jim Emmett, his two sons and two hired men. They were all Mormons. Grey wrote to Dolly, "You ought to see this crowd of Mormons I'm going with. If they aren't a tough bunch I never saw one. They all pack guns. But they're nice fellows."[122]

Jim Emmett had been accused of cattle rustling and was in Flagstaff for his trial, which had just ended. It was reported in the *Coconino Sun* of April 11, 1907, as follows: "The case of the Territory vs. James S. and William Emett* was one that attracted the attention of outsiders and during the trial the court-room was filled with those who wished to hear the evidence. The parties were charged with stealing and killing one red cow, the property of B.F. Saunders. . . .

*Various spellings of this man's name occur: Emmett, Emett, and Emet.

It took nearly two days time in which to try the case, and there was a large number of witnesses.... It was a hard fought case on both sides."[123]

Actually "only one of the Emmett cases was tried, the others were dismissed by the district attorney, the evidence in all cases being similar."[124]

These cases had been before the court since April 1905, and had attracted wide attention of the people in the county, rustling not being considered a minor offense in cattle country. The cases had been vigorously prosecuted and vigorously defended and expensive for both Mr. Saunders and the county, but as the newspaper stated, "alleged cattle stealing cases have to be tried, no matter what the cost may be."[125]

Their would-be companion still failing to show, the party left Flagstaff early of a morning. "Grey mounted the first horse he had been on in many years. To put it bluntly, Grey had never ridden anything but a farm plug back in Ohio."[126] Agonizing though it was, he hung to the pommel of his saddle through the long grueling days of their travel, until he became accustomed to this means of Western transportation.

By the time they reached the Colorado (a three-day ride), "The . . . River was high and swift, and Grey did not think they would be able to cross it, but they soon reached a cable strung across the river. Under it ran a rope.

"Across the river an old flat scow was moored to the bank. Jim Emmett fired his rifle, and a man appeared and got into a small skiff. He rowed upstream for a considerable distance, then swung into the current. The little skiff was twice turned around but reached the near bank safely. Two Mormons got in, recrossed the river and got into the scow. They grasped the rope overhead and began to pull. Slowly the scow came across the swift-running river.

"Jones, looking at Grey's taut face, said that they should get the agony over quickly. Horses were loaded aboard, the men climbed on, and the hazardous crossing was begun. Two or three times the scow was virtually swamped. Emmett was wet to the waist from trying to hold the horses and gear, which were in danger of being lost several times. Grey remarked that he must be a splendid swimmer or he would not take such chances. Emmett told him that he couldn't swim a stroke, and even if he could, it would not save him if he fell into the torrent."[127]

Thus Zane Grey crossed at Lee's Ferry. The first book to come out of this trip, where he listened to tales, absorbed dialect, learned of the West, and made copious notes on everything he heard or saw, was his biography of Jones, *The Last of the Plainsmen*. It was rejected by the publishers. Disappointed, but inspired with his Western experience, Grey's first Western novel, *The Heritage of the Desert*, was published in 1910. Labeled by his biographer, Frank Gruber, as the pattern for all of Zane Grey's Western novels, there are in it Mormon patriarchs, outlaws, and Indians, and in it also is a location where the old Mormon, August Naab, lives, that is more than faintly reminiscent of the river at Lee's Ferry.

Jacob Hamblin

Though exploration of the Colorado River is first associated with Powell, plaudits for the exploration of the southern Utah-northern Arizona region very likely should go to Jacob Hamblin. Little known outside Mormon County,

Jacob Vernon Hamblin, Utah's "Leatherstocking," 1819-1886—*Courtesy Arizona Historical Society*

Hamblin was one of the key explorers of what Powell called the "Plateau Province." Dedicated, responsible, knowledgeable, he was a man of the church whose leadership and explorative ventures created for the Mormons a Southern Road, making possible the colonization of the valley of the Little Colorado and the tributaries of the Gila.

His party had, in 1858, been the first white men to cross at Ute Ford since Father Escalante. He had also found a crossing below Grand Wash Cliffs at the lower end of Grand Canyon. In November 1859, he crossed the river near the mouth of the Paria, swimming over horses and mules. Later this would be known as Lee's Ferry. It is believed to be the first time the river was crossed at that point by anyone other than Indians.

Hamblin, as leader of his party, found this crossing on his second religious mission to the Hopi, a tribe in which the Mormon Church had great interest. Among the many legends laid over the Hopi people is one that they are descendents of the Nephites driven out by the Lamanites as told in the Book of Mormon. Another is that they are "white Indians" of Welsh ancestry, a story which has long made the rounds in American folklore. On Hamblin's first expedition to the Hopi in 1858, he had brought with him a Welsh Mormon who was left there to check as best he could for Welsh words in the Hopi language. Too, the Mormons were interested in converting the Hopi people to their own way of life.

During the following years, Hamblin made many crossings at the Paria by different means: by swimming over on horses, by a boat which was reassembled at the Paria Crossing; he even notes on one occasion "our luggage went over on rafts made of flatwood fastened together by withes."[128]

Hamblin knew Lee, had sent grape cuttings and coffee to him at the Paria; the crossing, of course, he could claim as his own. He knew the Hopi well and had taken Chief Tuba and his wife Pulaskanimki to his home in Utah by way of the Crossing of the Fathers. As Indian Agent he knew the Indians of this area: the Shivwits, Uinkarets, the Santa Claras, the Kaibabs.

Hamblin had worked as a kind of guide for Major Powell, bringing in supplies, and he was also his contact with the Mormon community. Of his relationship with Indians, Powell wrote glowingly of his Mormon friend, "Hamblin speaks their language well, and has a great influence over all the Indians in the region round about. He is a silent, reserved man, and when he speaks, it is in a slow quiet way that inspires great awe. His talk is so low that they must listen attentively to hear, and they sit around him in deathlike silence."[129]

Admittedly, at this time Powell knew nothing of Indian etiquette and so might attribute magical powers to Hamblin, but Hamblin himself knew his real power with Indians came from their trust of him. In a revelation he had been told if he never shed Indian blood, no Indian would ever shed his. He was a bulwark in his Mormon community, understanding or at least trying to understand his people's indignation over Indian depredations, and yet building, with infinite patience and no anger, a peaceful commitment with the Indian people.

In October 1870, lumber for a boat was lashed to mule backs and carried to the mouth of the Paria. There the boat was completed; and Powell, along with Hamblin, crossed the river and visited with the Hopi villages where Powell procured an abundance of articles for the Smithsonian. They then went on to Fort Defiance for a peace conference with the Navajos over pillaging sorties they had made against the Mormon villages. The Indians had gathered at the fort to receive rations and annuities. When their train from the Hopi villages arrived on October 30, Powell wrote that it was a wild spectacle.

Though it is doubted that Powell had any official capacity for being there, the pact that was eventually negotiated was one that outlawed raiding but welcomed the Navajos to the Mormon settlements for trading forays. It was signed on November 5.

In the winter of 1873-74, Hamblin, with the assistance of a Paiute, sought out the Southern Road to the headwaters of the Little Colorado, and the migration to Arizona truly began. Beale's Road, laid out in 1857 from Fort Defiance to the Colorado River, and following roughly the thirty-fifth parallel, was also used by the Mormons as part of their Southern Road. In 1874 about one hundred wagons were fitted out and crossed at Lee's Ferry to settle on the Little Colorado or the Tributaries of the Gila. Some followed Hamblin's road from Lee's Ferry through the Painted Desert to Grand Falls and along Beale's Road to the Little Colorado.

The Navajos had long had an extensive trade with the Mormon people, the principal items of exchange being blankets for horses. Hamblin, in the winter of 1874-75, assisted in carrying on a trading venture with the Navajos at Lee's Ferry. In the fall of 1874 there was considerable trouble with the Navajos and a "fort" was built at the Ferry on Hamblin's orders. It was used as a trading post but could also be used, if necessary, for defense. This was but four years after he had negotiated the treaty at Fort Defiance.

Once the crossing that he had made so often almost claimed his life. This was in May of 1876; two wagons with all their valuables were lost, three wagons and some luggage being on the ferry at the time. Brother Lorenzo W. Roundy was lost in this accident, his death being reported by Hamblin in the *Deseret News*. Brother Roundy's death was the first ever to be recorded there.

So Jacob, too, had a life at the Ferry, but six years after his trading venture, Hamblin embarked on yet another mission for his church. Thus, two who had come west with the first of the faithful now left the Colorado Plateau—Lee, whose life had sometimes been intertwined with that of Jacob Hamblin, was shot by the firing squad on March 23, 1877; Hamblin left to carry on the work of his church with the Apaches in Arizona. He worked in this endeavor for five years, dying in Pleasanton, New Mexico, in 1886. His body was later moved to Alpine, Arizona, where it was again interred. Sometimes called The Leatherstocking of Utah, Jacob Hamblin, who had contributed so greatly to our knowledge of the Plateau Province, was buried far from the place he knew so well.

Warren M. Johnson

Warren M. Johnson was the man the church appointed to take over the ferry when Lee was arrested. For twenty years thereafter he and his family were at the crossing. They were recalled by many of the river followers as

According to Frank Johnson, who is the baby in his mother's arms, this photograph was taken by Buffalo Bill's photographer who visited the Johnson ranch in 1893. This was just prior to the time Warren Johnson was recalled from his twenty year mission to the Indians. It was a mission on which he had been sent by Brigham Young and included taking over the ranch from Emma Lee and operating the ferry. (From information on the original photograph)— *Courtesy State Records Center and Archives, Santa Fe, New Mexico, E.R. Fryer Collection*

The Johnson house and part of Lee's Ferry ranch as it appeared in 1893...the house was destroyed by fire in the 1920's.—*Courtesy State Records Center and Archives, Santa Fe, New Mexico, E.R. Fryer Collection*

Close-up view of the Johnson house at Lee's Ferry.—*Courtesy State Records Center and Archives, Santa Fe, New Mexico, E.R. Fryer Collection*

hospitable people who ran the ferry effectively, with few losses of property and no loss of life.

In 1874, after Lee's departure, the Mormons set up a trading post at the ferry devoted to Navajo trade. As late as the 1930s there were Indians who remembered "riding to Lee's Ferry to barter blankets and silverwork for horses, flour and syrup."[130]

To the Navajos, the name for the crossing had always been *to ha' naant' eetiin,* or "Crossing against the current." "After the ferry started, Navajos began to trade blankets for horses and gave the place the new name of *tsinaa' ee dahsi' ani,* 'Where the boat sits.'"[131]

A post office was established at the ferry in 1879, and Johnson was the postmaster. There was one there for forty-four years, until March 2, 1923, when it was discontinued.

When the ferry was sold by the Grand Canyon Cattle Company, the farm at Lonely Dell was purchased by the sons of Warren Johnson.

Buffalo Bill

During his flamboyant lifetime, William Frederick Cody was a pony express rider, an army scout, a buffalo hunter. He was a rancher and a developer of

This photograph of Buffalo Bill and his party was made in the fall of 1892 as they crossed at Lee's Ferry on their way to the Kaibab.—*Courtesy Special Collections Division, Northern Arizona University Library, Edward T. Lamb Collection*

the Big Horn Basin. It is, however, as a wild West showman that he is best remembered. And he did have an association, however minute, with Lee's Ferry.

The Golden Jubilee of Queen Victoria was in the year 1887, and Buffalo Bill and his entourage went to England as a part of the American Exhibition.[132] Wherever they went, their reception was warm and exciting. Earl's Court was the place to be that summer. It teemed with London society and theatrical folk. "The place was crawling with toffs, awash in gray toppers, ablaze with diamond-studded honorables and dames and ladies of the realm."[133] The Prince of Wales came, the Princesses Victoria, Louise and Maude, the Crown

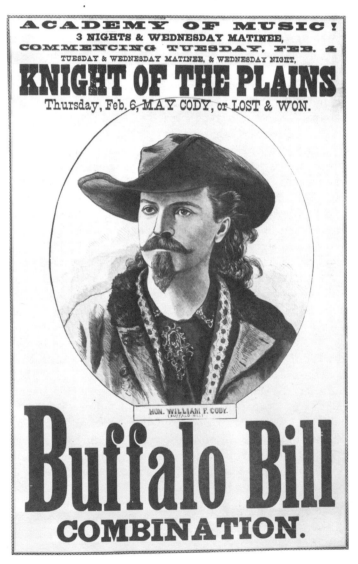

Playbill advertising *May Cody; or Lost and Won;* commissioned by Buffalo Bill, the background of the play was the Mountain Meadows Massacre.— *Courtesy Buffalo Bill Historical Center, Cody, Wyoming*

Prince of Denmark, and there was a command performance for the marvelous old Queen herself. Starring members of the company were presented to her.

Buffalo Bill, with his great charm and fascinating wild West show was now acquainted with the moneyed and titled of Britain, but he was also acquainted with the history of John D. Lee.

There had been much publicity in the East of the trial, subsequent conviction, and execution of Lee. Always on the alert for the timely, Cody commissioned Major Andrew Sheridan Burt[134] of the U.S. Army to write a play about it. The result was *May Cody; or, Lost and Won*. The background of the play was the Mountain Meadows Massacre. May Cody, Buffalo Bill's sister, was heroine of the play, though she had never been anywhere near the disaster. Her part was played by the actress Constance Hamblin. Apparently unrelated to Jacob Hamblin, it is interesting to note the name once again was associated with that of Lee.

At the Bowery Theatre on September 3, 1877, with much prepublicity, Cody opened *Lost and Won* to record crowds. "It was the best drama I had yet produced," he said, "and proved a grand success both financially and artistically."[135]

In 1889 the show was again in Europe, this time on the Continent; in 1890 they winter-quartered in Strasbourg, Germany; in 1891 they went from St. Petersburg to Glasgow, and again to London where they gave a command performance for the Queen on the grounds of Windsor Castle. On this last trip to England, Cody met John W. Young, a son of the Mormon leader Brigham Young and a representative of the Mormon Church in Britain. Young was a promoter and likely foresaw the American preoccupation with royalty. Leastways, he conceived a grandiose scheme of making the Kaibab a hunting and travel center for English nobility. His plan was to have grand lodges and hotels erected, as well as staging hunts on a splendid scale. Some English sportsmen entertained the idea favorably and decided to make the trip to investigate possibilities. Buffalo Bill was persuaded by Young to recruit some of his new stock in the Kaibab, for the World's Columbian Exposition in Chicago was upcoming, and to act as a guide for the sportsmen interested in the venture.

In the fall of 1892, Utah representatives of the project took wagons to Flagstaff, Arizona, to meet Buffalo Bill and the Britishers at the railroad. They returned to the Kaibab by the way of Lee's Ferry and Houserock Valley. Buffalo Bill's party included Lords Ingram and Milmey; an English Major McKinnon; John Baker, the Cowboy Kid of the show, and a kind of adopted son of Buffalo Bill's; and the great showman himself.[136] Gazed at, looked over, royally entertained with Western hospitality, the Britishers nevertheless decided the Kaibab was too far from England for a hunting lodge, no matter how choice the scenery and the game.

One wonders if Buffalo Bill, crossing at the ferry, remembered John D. Lee, *Lost and Won,* and how it had opened to great crowds in New York City.

9.

Dams and River Water

The history of the arid Southwest is founded not on the land, but on water, and because of it few rivers have had a history of more importance than the Colorado. Found a year before Desoto discovered the Mississippi, it was never of its own accord a generous patron of mankind; its waterway did not carry men to new lands to till as did the Ohio; it did not create a delta land to succor its people with splendid fields; neither cities of industry nor commerce sprang up along its banks. It was miserly and truculent, demanding the most of men.

For these reasons it has long been a river of controversy. The waters of no other river in our country have aroused such rancor between states, there has been rivalry and much argument over where dams should be located along its watercourse or whether there should be dams at all. What it was not of its own accord, man has attempted to make it. Few waterways have had a more human history, unless it is the Nile, with which it is often compared. The Nile (source of Kagera to the sea) is 3,946 miles; the Colorado (source of the Green to the Gulf) is only 1,700 miles, but the fall in the Colorado from the source to the mouth is 14,000 feet, more than doubling that of the Nile, which is 6,600 feet.

The drainage of the Colorado for the sake of its politics and from a geological, economic, and hydrological point of view, divides itself naturally into two basins. The upper basin consists of the states of Colorado, New Mexico, Utah, and Wyoming, while the lower basin comprises the states of Arizona, California, and Nevada.

For fifteen years, from 1905-1920, devastating floods inundated the Imperial Valley of California, and there was great political pressure for the building of a dam on the Colorado as a flood control measure. In addition, the river was seen as a means of making the Southwestern economy boom, the region even then being seen as a comer.

The U.S. Geological Survey, responsible for dam locations, was assigned to investigate for possible dam sites. It was in the position as U.S.G.S. hydrologist that Eugene Clyde LaRue came to know Lee's Ferry. The Southern California Edison Company was interested in cheap electric power for that rapidly growing area, and in a rare display of government and private endeavor these two cooperated on an expedition in 1921 to do topographic mapping of the canyon. The Kolb brothers were among the boatmen for this venture.

Because of the various proposals on the utilization of the river's waters, the Colorado River Commission met in Santa Fe, New Mexico, in November of 1922. For fifteen days they argued, discussed, compromised, and in the end came up with what has become known as the Colorado River Compact. Building on the natural division of the river, they officially divided the Colorado basin into the upper and lower, the dividing line between the two being drawn at Lee's Ferry (Colorado River Mile 0). Though an imaginary line, it brought Lee's Ferry into focus again as a place of historical significance in the Southwest. The Compact left "the states of each basin to work out the ultimate distribution among themselves."[137]

From Mile 0 all river miles up or downstream were measured by their distance from the Ferry mark. A gauging station had previously been installed at the Ferry to measure the flow of the river.

The Commission was chaired by then Secretary of Commerce, Herbert Hoover. At the meeting, Hoover said, "It is far more to the interest of America that we should develop homes out under the blue skies than that we should stifle our agriculture for the benefit of our industry."[138] Indeed, the principles by which the Commission was guided was that flood control was the first to be considered, then irrigation, and only lastly power. Interestingly, it was established that "in paying for this development, the order was reversed. That is to say, the sale of power shall bear the bulk of the burden, with irrigation and flood control to be assessed for a share only in the event power proves unable to carry the whole load."[139]

The Compact was argued over, ratified by the state legislature with the exception of one, rewritten by the other six when Arizona refused ratification, hassled over in the Congress, appealed to the courts, but eventually sanctioned; the building of Boulder Dam was the initial step of the Colorado River Project.

From 1921 until 1928, the hydrologist LaRue fought a losing battle to have a dam in the upper reaches of the canyon built first. His choice was Mile 4 damsite in Glen Canyon, that is, 4 miles upstream from Lee's Ferry. He called it the Lee's Ferry Dam. This dam, according to his projections, would be three hundred twenty feet high and store eight million feet of water.

Ten years before Boulder was dedicated, the first excursion boat had been on the the Colorado. It is generally conceded to be the Todd-Page party of 1926. And in November of the following year, a party of professional photographers from Pathé left Green River and were at Lee's Ferry within the month. During the thirties, river running came to be the thing to do for the adventurous. The honor of being the first women to traverse the canyon from Green River, Utah, to Boulder City goes to Elzada U. Clover and Lois Jotter. This was in June of 1938. They camped at Lee's Ferry where two of their boatmen left and two others had to be recruited. They were on a Norman Davies Nevills expedition. Nevills ran river boat operations and was sometimes called the "Wrangler of the River." He was killed when his plane crashed into a cliff in September of 1949.

The first woman to try running the canyons was a pert, twenty-two-year-old French sportswoman, Genevieve de Colmont, who with her husband, Bernard, and a friend Antoine de Seynes, left Green River, Wyoming, on September 13,

A grouping of "river people". . . Left to right: Norman Nevills, Blanche Kolb (Mrs. Emery Kolb), Lorin Bell, Edith Kolb Lehnert (daughter of Blanche and Emery Kolb), Bill Gibson, Lois Jotter, Dr. Elzada Clover, Emery Kolb. Lois Jotter and Dr. Elzada Clover were the first women with Nevills on the river.—*Courtesy Northern Arizona University on behalf of the Kolb Collection, Copyright 1977 by Emery Lehnert.*

Norman Nevills in 1947. His boat *Wen* was on its fifth trip through Grand Canyon.—*Courtesy National Park Service, photographer: J.M. Eden*

Foldboat Trip Down Colorado Described by Parisian and Wife

Explorer Says She Is First Woman to Conquer River in Any Kind of Boat; 900-Mile Journey in 16-Foot Craft Took Two Months

The story of the first foldboat trip through the Colorado River rapids was told yesterday by Bernard de Colmont, of Paris, France, who made the first trip with his wife, Genevieve de Colmont, and a friend, Antoine de Seynes, also of Paris. Mrs. de Colmont is the only woman on record who has navigated a boat of any kind down the Colorado River.

The 900-mile trip started in the middle of September at Green River, Wyo., and ended two months later in Arizona, 200 miles upstream from Boulder Dam. Since then Mr. de Seynes has sailed for France, and the de Colmonts, after traveling in the West, drove to New York, arriving about ten days ago. They are now visiting friends, Mr. and Mrs. Dee Mills, of 1146 Dean Street, Brooklyn, and expect to sail for France within the next two weeks.

Mr. de Colmont, who is associated with the Paris Museum of Natural History and has made two previous field expeditions to America for the museum, was reticent on the records set on the trip. "We didn't come here to break any records," he said. "We came to test our boats, not for commercial purposes, but in relation to problems of exploration."

Several "Firsts"

Finally, Mr. de Colmont smiled and said, "I know you like in this country to talk about the first and the biggest, so I will tell you that this was the first time this trip has been made in this kind of boat, and my wife was the first woman who ever tried to go in her own boat. Only two other women have gone before, and they went only in the lower part of the river and they were passengers."

Each member of the party had his own sixteen-foot foldboat, a boat with a collapsible wooden framework and a covering of rubberized fabric. The entire boat weighs only fifty pounds, and can be folded up in three pieces, the heaviest of which weighs twenty pounds.

Mr. de Colmont explained that he wished to test the boats as a means of reducing the element of chance in the field of exploration. When an explorer meets rapids, he must either shoot them or portage, and if his boats are heavy and the shore rough and stony, it may be physically impossible to make a portage. With the foldboat, it is easy to make a portage around the dangerous rapids, no matter how rough the shore.

River Best for Tests

"We chose the Colorado River," Mr. de Colmont said, "because it was the worst for rapids and the most interesting we could find. They say there are 365 big rapids and twice as many small ones, but we didn't stop to count. Most of the time it was just one rapid after another. It was either that or dead water—there was no happy medium."

The party made only one portage, around the worst rapids of the trip, in Cataract Canyon, just below the confluence of the Green and Colorado Rivers in Utah. The foldboats were superior to heavy wooden boats in shooting rapids, Mr. de Colmont said, because if one were swept onto a rock it was swept right off again, whereas a heavier boat might get jammed on a rock and take four or five men to pull it off.

There was only one accident in the entire 900 miles, and that was when Mr. de Seynes's boat struck a rock. The fabric did not break, but several of the ribs of the boat were broken. The boat was pulled up on shore, the breaks were repaired with driftwood, and the party moved on. "Once you start on that trip, you have to go on, with no possibility of getting out of the canyon," Mr. de Colmont said. "It is not because the cliffs are too sheer, but it is no use to climb the cliffs because it is too difficult to get across country to a highway."

The first part of the trip was down the Green River, which flows south from Wyoming into Utah, bends eastward into Colorado and then back into Utah and joins the Colorado River. The course then was down the Colorado into Arizona and through the Grand Canyon. It had been planned to end the trip at Boulder Dam, but when the party came within 200 miles of it, they found the river frozen. They waited two weeks and the river was still frozen, so they gave up the venture.

Collected Insects

Along the way Mr. de Colmont collected insects for his museum. He snared 200 specimens, and found that the varieties differed widely in the different sections of the trip. He said that since he is not an entomologist, he would have to study his collection with the aid of an expert before he could attempt to evaluate it.

"We had no narrow escapes," Mr. de Colmont said, "but that is just wha we wanted to avoid. So there is nothing very thrilling in the trip. The idea was to limit the part of chance as much as possible. We are still alive and safe, and we still have the boats in good condition. That shows that the boats are good for the Colorado River—so they are good for almost any river in the world."

Mrs. de Colmont displayed a pink oilcloth pig, her mascot on the trip. Mr. de Colmont said that he had carried a brown oilcloth bear in his boat, and explained that the popularity of foldboats for sport and recreation in France had led to the appearance on the market of waterproof "mascots."

Mrs. de Colmont then produced a live baby alligator, eight inches long, and two baby turtles, about the size of a silver dollar, named, respectively, Cocoanut, Peanut and Doughnut. The de Colmonts bought these pets in Hollywood, brought them east in their automobile and intend to take them home to Paris.

This clipping from the *New York Herald Tribune* regarding the Colorado River journey of Genevieve De Colmont, her husband Bernard, and Antoine de Seynes is from the files in the Library of the National Park Service, Grand Canyon, Arizona and is reproduced here through their courtesy.

Alexander E. (Zee) Grant in the kayak *Escalante*, running the river in July, 1941. The kayak travelled with Norman Nevills and two cataract boats.—
Courtesy National Park Service, photographer: Weldon Heald

1938, in three folding kayaks, reportedly more afraid of the water than the river. Well into the journey de Seynes' boat sustained severe damage when it was swept onto the rocks. The three got it on shore where they found several of its ribs broken, but the fabric still intact. They repaired the ribs with driftwood and continued on their way. They all left the river at Lee's Ferry in early November without attempting Marble or Grand Canyon. Other early kayakers were Charles Fulton Man, who made it to Lee's Ferry in 1939, and Alexander "Zee" Grant who made the first kayak run through Grand Canyon.

In 1938, the first inflated rubber boat was brought to the river by Haldane "Buzz" Holmstrom. His boat was "sixteen feet long, with a beam of five and a half feet." It weighed eighty-three pounds and "was the first inflated rubber equipment on the river."[140] Holmstrom had in October of 1937 made it alone from Green River to Hoover Dam in a sixteen foot boat of the Galloway-Stone pattern.

"By June, 1940, when Bert Loper and Laphene (Don) Harris came down the river trailing the first Green-Colorado expedition of Norman Nevills, river excursions had come to be so common they hardly warranted attention or counting."[141]

In 1921, when the Colorado Commission met, the principles by which they were guided was that flood control was to be considered first, then irrigation, and lastly power. With the tremendous increase in Southwestern population, with the expansion of industry, there has been an almost complete inversion. Many now consider the development of power to be the foremost consideration in dam construction on the river. And in its politics, its settlements, the division of its waters are still contended. But nowhere within their orbit could the Commission see the great demand for recreational areas.

They could not foresee the growing popularity of fishing, boating, camping, hunting, hiking; they could not imagine the number of bird-watchers or wildlife and flower enthusiasts who would roam the waters and lakeshores made by the dams on the Colorado. They could not imagine that Congress, in a different time, would have these same lakes and shores proclaimed National Recreational Areas. They could not fathom that the lake borders would be studded with boat launching ramps and gas stations, eating places, and small stores that do a thriving business as purveyors of camp supplies. That for a demanding public there would be built picnic places, campgrounds, swimming beaches, and that thousands of boats would ply the canyons whose waters had been made easy, but where once river explorers portaged and struggled to make a way.

For a new breed has come to the river. They do not belong to the time of the explorer, they do not serve as officials of government, nor do they seek wealth in the sands or on the ledges of the river. They love the river for itself and they come in ever-increasing numbers—they come for the daring, the adventuring, and for the quiet it sometimes still offers.

In lieu of all of this, it seems incomprehensible that only a little over one hundred years ago, Lieutenant Joseph Christmas Ives in his *Report Upon the Colorado River of the West,* could have written, "Ours has been the first, and doubtless will be the last party of whites to visit this profitless locality. It seems intended by nature that the Colorado River, along the greater portion

Bert Loper in 1949, the year of his death.—*Courtesy Arizona Historical Society*

of its lonely and majestic way, shall be forever unvisited and undisturbed." [142]

Boulder Dam proved its worth by feeding the lights of Southern California and making green the Imperial Valley. Dams, levies, ditches, canals, and aqueducts funneled its waters to places far distant from the river. What one had made good, man reasoned, many would make better. And so he dug, blasted, drained, rerouted, cemented, rocked, diverted, and each time another dam was wedged between the banks, he controlled more and more the venerable old river.

In view of the great demand of the populace for harnessing it back in the 1920s, the Commission would perhaps find it hardest of all to believe that, in this time, preservationists lament the passing of the Colorado as a free river and raise their voices in the halls of Congress against the building of more dams.

When a new dam was considered for an upper canyon site, LaRue's Mile 4 site was again rejected due to poor foundation conditions and other considerations, economic and scientific. [143] As the new dam was being surveyed, the crews worked out of Lee's Ferry and lived in the rock cabins, some of which were among the seven built by Spencer for bunkhouses, lab, blacksmith, and mess hall.

The first major construction was started on Glen Canyon Dam October 2, 1956, but its roots go back to 1922, for its reservoir will help provide holdover reserves of water to meet the terms of the Colorado River Basin compact.

With all the excursions and all the activity, the number of people who have lost their lives on the river is relatively low. Out of a total of fifty* since

* in a hundred year span, 1869-1969 (Reilly, P.T. "How Deadly is Big Red")

Glen Canyon Dam, Colorado River Storage Project, Utah-Arizona. The waters below Glen Canyon Dam may be reached by boaters putting in at Lee's Ferry, 15 river miles below the dam.—*Courtesy U.S. Department of the Interior, Bureau of Reclamation, P.O. Box 11568, Salt Lake City, Utah, 84111*

River view, Lee's Ferry.—*Courtesy Northern Arizona Pioneers' Historical Society Collection, Special Collections Division, Northern Arizona University Library*

Charles R. Savage had a photography shop and gallery in Salt Lake City. It was in the Savage gallery that Powell met James Fennemore who later became a photographer with the second expedition. See Endnote 36.—*Courtesy Arizona Historical Society*

1869, twelve died at Lee's Ferry, making it the most dangerous place on the river. Of the twelve, ferry accidents claimed the lives of seven, two incidents of skiffs overturning took the lives of four, and one incident of a canoe capsizing took the life of another. The latter occurred at the lower ferry site. [144]

Before the construction of the dam, river trips used to end at the north bank of Lee's Ferry, and Grand Canyon trips were initiated from there. It is a far cry from the twenty to thirty boats observed at Lee's Ferry in 1897, the hundreds of skiffs in the slow water during the great gold flurry, to operations like Norman Davies Nevills and those of the Rainbow Bridge-Monument Valley Expeditions that operated trips from Copper Canyon to Lee's Ferry in the early thirties, to the great influx of people who go on river trips today. Gaylord Staveley, professional river runner, son-in-law of Norman Nevills, and owner of the river expeditions his father-in-law started, estimates that twenty thousand people have traveled the canyon (1971).* Controversy now rages over the environmental impact of the great number of people who go through the canyon, which though rockbound and recalcitrant in her ways, is delicately fragile in her needs.

Consider these two descriptions of Lee's Ferry. One was written in 1869 by E.G. Woolley[145] who, at twenty-five, was adjutant of the Iron County Militia, out to intercept Navajos who had stolen stock from the southern settlements of Utah. He wrote, "The water runs swift, looking quite rough, and we can hear the roaring of the water from where we stand." They were on a precipice directly opposite and six hundred feet above the junction of the Colorado and Paria Rivers. He declared it a "magnificent view." The other is a moving portrait written after the intrusion of Glen Canyon Dam, "The water flowing by is now liquid emerald, but it moves too languidly to catch diamonds of sunlight. Its surface is lifeless almost like a picture of water, rather than water. From habit one refers to it as 'the river' but it is not any more; it is 'waste water' from Glen Canyon Dam. The river was a feverish, silt-laden Presence that through late spring and summer welled to flow over the toes of our willow tree and urgently on into Marble Canyon. The waste-water river doesn't do that; there's not enough of it. All its spirit seems to have been absorbed by its plunge against the vanes of the dam's hydropower generators. It even permits slimy green moss to grow on its rocks, something the rushing, rasping old Colorado would never have allowed."[146]

Changed it is. The flags of the excursion boats are only faintly reminiscent of those made by Ellen Thompson for the boats of Powell, built so sturdily, so heavy and cumbersome. Neoprene rafts have followed the war surplus pontoons.

Glen Canyon, 15.3 miles upstream from Lee's Ferry, brought a new kind of life to the old site. The river's waters are stocked with fish, it has become an area where people come to cast their lines; it is the pushoff point for the many trips through Grand Canyon.

Yet in a way, one likes to feel it is keened to the almost forgotten past: the time when Navajos in white breeches and red leggings called out to be rowed across; when the Mormon settlements of lower Utah were not linked by farm-to-

---

* in 1980 alone, the number was estimated to be 12,000 people.

market roads; when expeditions were not made solely for the love of adventure.

One likes to think it lives on its past, on an air of mystery, bearing a name that speaks eloquently of a stalwart pioneer and yet stained with a scar of shame; that it is a place reminiscent of a time when hates were violent but endeavor and individualism were respected. Hovering over the camper's fire are the spectres of Fathers Escalante and Dominguez; of Jacob Hamblin and Powell's men; Stanton's party and Mormon pioneers, John D. Lee and those Indians who first brought the white men to the river. In places, rapids are still swift; and visitors, for whatever cause they come, marvel at the canyons and the beauty the river has made. The seeker knows the legends it has secreted, and those who love the river best hearken always to the story of Lonely Dell, which we know as Lee's Ferry, a crossing on the Colorado, and once the gateway to the pioneer Southwest.

Endnotes

---

[1] Mountain Meadows, located 35 miles from Cedar City in southwestern Utah, had long been known as a resting place for travelers to the West. It was high and cool, the elevation being about 6000 feet. There was forage and water for cattle. It was here that the massacre occurred in 1857 (Juanita Brooks, *The Mountain Meadows Massacre*).

[2] Hernán Cortés was born in 1485 in Medellin. He left Spain in 1504 bound for the Indian Islands and aided Diego Velasquez in the conquest of Cuba in 1511. Chosen by Velasquez to command the expedition to "New Spain," he took his departure on February 18, 1519, and thus began the Conquest of Mexico.

[3] Francisco Vázquez de Coronado, native of Salamanca, came to America in 1535 as a member of Viceroy Mendoza's retinue. He was appointed governor of the province of Nueva Galicia on the western frontier when he was only twenty-eight years old. When news of riches to the north were brought back by Fray Marcos, an army was formed to explore the land called Cibola. Coronado was appointed Captain-General. He left Compostela on February 3, 1540, for the long march into what is now New Mexico.

[4] Hawikuh is located some 13 miles southwest of Zuñi Pueblo. Extensive excavations were accomplished at this pueblo between 1917 and 1923 by Dr. Frederick W. Hodge under the auspices of the Museum of American Indians, Heye Foundation.

[5] Garcia López de Cárdenas was a cavalry captain in Coronado's army. He came to America in 1535, going first to South America and Cuba before settling in Mexico. He soon became a member of the viceroy's staff and spent several years in government service before becoming a part of Coronado's staff.

Cárdenas was married to Doña Ana de Mendoza of an aristocratic Spanish family and a distant relative of Viceroy Mendoza.

[6] Sea of Cortés bounded eastward by the mainland of Mexico, westward by Baja California and opening at the bottom to the Pacific Ocean; this body of water is known on most maps as the Gulf of California. It was discovered by Francisco de Ulloa, relative of Cortés, in 1539.

[7] George Parker Winship, *The Coronado Expedition, 1540-1542;* Translation of Castañeda, p. 209.

[8] Garcés, Spanish Franciscan priest, was born April 12, 1738, in a province of northern Spain which was also the homeland of Henry VIII's wife, Catherine of Aragon. He came to San Xavier del Bac in 1768. San Xavier was the northernmost of the Sonora missions. From here he ministered to the Papagos, the Pimas, and later to the Yumas. An inveterate traveler, he wandered far from his mission home, west to the Colorado River where he visited the Havasupai in the Grand Canyon and the Hopis in their villages, on to California, always looking for new mission roads. In 1781 he died a martyr's death at the newly established mission near old Fort Yuma.

[9] Fray Silvestre Velez de Escalante, was a Spanish priest and member of the teaching and missionary order founded by St. Francis of Assisi, Italy, in the twelfth century.

Others in the expedition were Fray Francisco Atanasio Dominguez, superior of the Franciscan Missions in New Mexico; Don Bernardo Miera y Pacheco, astronomer and cartographer; Don Pedro Cisneros, Alcalde of the Pueblo of Zuñi; Don Joaquín Lain, citizen of Zuñi; Lorenzo Olivares of El Paso; two brothers, Lucrecio and Andrés Muñiz (interpreter); Juan de Aguilar, and Simón Lucero.

[10] Elliott Coues, *On the Trail of a Spanish Pioneer, Garces Diary, 1775-76*, p. 231.

[11] *El Vado de los Padres*, Crossing of the Fathers, a historical point where Fathers Escalante and Dominguez and their party crossed the river in 1776. This crossing is a short distance above the Utah-Arizona line. Later the Mormons sometimes crossed here when going south into Arizona.

[12] "The Paria River rises in the Escalante Mountains in Garfield County, Utah, flows southeasterly through Kane County into Arizona, and joins the Colorado at a point 31 miles below the Utah-Arizona line. The total area of the basin is 1,440 square miles." E.C. LaRue, *Colorado River and Its Utilization, Water Supply Paper 395*, p. 93.

[13] Rachel Andora Woolsey was born August 5, 1825, and died in 1912 in Lebanon, Arizona. She was married to Lee on May 3, 1845, in Nauvoo, Illinois. She was Lee's sixth wife and mother of eight of his children. Rachel was sister to his first wife, Aggatha Ann Woolsey (Juanita Brooks, *John Doyle Lee, Zealot-Pioneer Builder-Scapegoat*).

[14] Aggatha Ann Woolsey was born January 18, 1814, Lincoln County, Kentucky and died June 4, 1886, New Harmony, Utah. She was married to Lee on July 24, 1833. She was the first wife of John D. Lee and mother of eleven of his children (Juanita Brooks, *John Doyle Lee, Zealot-Pioneer Builder-Scapegoat*).

[15] Emma Batchelor (sometimes spelled Batchelder or Bachellor), seventeenth wife of John D. Lee, was born April 21, 1836, at Uckfield, Sussex Co., England. She had seven children by Lee and died in Winslow, Arizona on November 16, 1897. (Juanita Brooks, *John Doyle Lee, Zealot-Pioneer Builder-Scapegoat* and Juanita Brooks, *Emma Lee*).

[16] John Doyle Lee, *A Mormon Chronicle, the Diaries of John D. Lee, 1848-1876*, edited and annotated by Robert Glass Cleland and Juanita Brooks (San Marino, Calif.: Huntington Library, 1955), vol. II, p. 181.

[17] Jacob's Pools. Named for Jacob Hamblin, these pools are on the route used by Hamblin to reach the Hopi country. He is considered to be the first white man to camp at this place (Will C. Barnes, *Arizona Place Names*).

[18] Jim Bridger went with General William H. Ashley's second expedition to the Rockies when he was only seventeen years old. Some historians credit him with the discovery of the Great Salt Lake in 1825. He was at one time a part owner of the Rocky Mountain Fur Company and established Fort Bridger on the Central Overland Trail. His post became a stopover for travelers to Oregon and California. Bridger was a renowned trapper, a famed storyteller, well-known trader, and a respected mountain man. He died in 1881, blind and old, in a Missouri community called Little Santa Fe.

[19] Brigham Young (1801-1877) was born in Vermont of Methodist background and was converted to Mormonism in Ohio in 1832. Practical, shrewd, enterprising, enthusiastic, of commanding presence, he quickly rose in the hierarchy of the Mormon Church, being ordained one of the Twelve Apostles in the year 1835. He was sent to preach in England in 1839 and was credited there with making thousands of converts for the church. Elected to succeed Joseph Smith, he exerted his great abilities as an organizer moving the Mormon people out of Illinois, and in stages, leading them westward, following the dream of their prophet Joseph Smith to found an independent state somewhere in the Rocky Mountain region. He was a strong leader of the Mormon Church and died in his beloved Salt Lake in August of 1877.

[20] Jacob Vernon Hamblin was born in Ohio in 1819 and came to Utah in 1850. Five years later he settled at Santa Clara on the Virgin River. In 1857 he was appointed president of the Mormon's Southern Indian Mission. He is credited with being the first white man to cross the Colorado River at Ute Ford after Father Escalante's expedition.

Hamblin also served as a guide for some of Powell's overland ventures. He died at Pleasanton, New Mexico, in 1886. His body was later moved to Alpine, Arizona, where it was again interred.

[21] John Doyle Lee, *A Mormon Chronicle, the Diaries of John D. Lee, 1848-1876*, edited and annotated by Robert Glass Cleland and Juanita Brooks (San Marino, Calif.: Huntington Library, 1955), vol. II, p. 184.

[22] James Buchanan (1791-1868), a Pennsylvanian, was the president to precede Abraham Lincoln. Elected on the Democratic party ticket, he served one term as President of the United States, 1857-1861.

[23] Haun's Mill Massacre, an affair in Missouri in 1838 in which seventeen Mormons were killed. The settlement was reportedly attacked by two hundred militiamen. Women and children were shot as they attempted to escape. Incidents of the militiamen killing the wounded were reported. Of the thirty-eight men and boys in the village, seventeen were slain and fifteen were wounded.

[24] Juanita Brooks, *The Mountain Meadows Massacre* (Stanford: Stanford University Press, 1950), p. 29.

[25] *Ibid.*, p. 41.

[26] John Cradlebaugh (1819-1872), a native of Ohio, was appointed United States Associate Justice for the district of Utah in June of 1858 and arrived there in November of the same year. Due to his relentless pursuit of the Mountain Meadows affair, he became a hated public official in Utah. Moving to Nevada, he was elected a delegate to the 37th Congress from that Territory and served from December 2, 1861 to May 3, 1863. During the Civil War he was a Colonel in the Union Army serving the One Hundredth and Fourteenth Regiment, Ohio Volunteer Infantry. He was wounded at Vicksburg and after his discharge entered the mining business in Nevada. He died in 1872 and was buried in Circlesville, Ohio, where he was born.

[27] John Wesley Powell (1834-1902) was born in the state of New York. Early in his life the family moved to Ohio where he was fortunate to come under the influence of George Crookham who was one of the best self-taught naturalists of his day, and had been an assistant in the first geological survey made in Ohio. He gave to Powell a lifelong interest which he pursued relentlessly, but always with an intuitive spirit. As a young man he made river trips on the Mississippi, the Ohio, the Illinois, the Des Moines. He was also a schoolteacher. Powell enlisted in the Union Army at the outbreak of the Civil War, and although he rose to the rank of Lieutenant Colonel, he retained the title of Major, and it is by that name we know him through the journals of the Colorado Expeditions. Powell lost his right forearm in the Battle of Shiloh in 1862. However, despite such a loss he remained in the army and was not discharged until January of 1865.

Powell became director of the Bureau of Ethnology and he also served as Director of the U.S. Geological Survey. Neil M. Judd, in his book *The Bureau of American Ethnology*, has called him "a geologist by profession and an anthropologist by preference."

Powell was married to his first cousin Emma Dean in 1861 and their only child, Mary Dean Powell was born in Salt Lake City in September 1871. Mrs. Powell accompanied her husband on many of his westward treks and is occasionally mentioned in the journals of the survey parties (William Culp Darrah, *Utah Historical Quarterly*, vol. XV, and Neil M. Judd, *The Bureau of American Ethnology*).

[28] Almon Harris Thompson was born in Stoddard, New Hampshire, September 24, 1839. He was married to Ellen L. Powell, sister of Major John Wesley Powell. During the Civil War he served as a First Lieutenant of the 139th Illinois Volunteer Infantry. He served as superintendent of schools in various Illinois communities and was at one time a curator of the Illinois Natural History Society. Known as "Prof" to his colleagues on the expedition, he was considered to be a kindly man of a generous turn of mind. In the diaries of the other members of the survey party, he was written and spoken of with

affection. Along with Powell and Hillers of the Second Expedition, he devoted the remainder of his life to public service and was Chief Geographer of the U.S. Geological Survey when he died in July of 1906 (Herbert E. Gregory, *Utah Historical Quarterly*, vol. VII).

[29] Frederick Samuel Dellenbaugh (1853-1935) was, at seventeen, the youngest member of the second Powell expedition down the Colorado River. He served as artist and assistant topographer and was a distant relative of A.H. Thompson. Twenty-eight years later he participated in extended exploration of Alaska and Siberia. During his life he had an outstanding career as writer, explorer, artist, topographer, mapmaker, and lecturer. During his later years, he was sometimes known as the "Grand Old Man of the Colorado," and indeed it is to him that we owe the most complete general account of the second expedition. Besides "A Canyon Voyage," which is their story, Dellenbaugh also wrote other books regarding the West and particularly about the country of the Colorado. He died in January 1935, one of the last two members of John Wesley Powell's Colorado River Expeditions.

[30] John K. Hillers (1843-1925), known as Jack to his companions, also sometimes called Bismarck, was born in Hanover, Germany. He had come to the United States in 1852 and served in the War Between the States and in Western outposts. Hillers was working as a teamster in Salt Lake City when he joined the Powell party in 1871 and gradually took over the photographic work of the second expedition. He was associated with Major Powell all of his remaining life in their work with the Geological Survey and the Bureau of Ethnology. Throughout their diaries the men refer to Hillers as the one who liked to sing.

[31] John Doyle Lee, *A Mormon Chronicle, The Diaries of John D. Lee, 1848-1876*, edited and annotated by Robert Glass Cleland and Juanita Brooks (San Marino, Calif.: Huntington Library, 1955), vol. II, p. 208.

[32] Ellen Powell Thompson was sister of Major Powell and wife of Almon Harris Thompson. She accompanied the party on some of their trips but generally headquartered at Kanab. Mrs. Thompson was well liked by members of the Colorado River Survey Party and is remembered for her good humor and gracious manners in their letters and memoirs.

[33] Harvey C. DeMotte was in the field with Powell in 1874 as a topographer. DeMotte was a personal friend of Powell's. He was also a mathematics professor at Wesleyan University in Bloomington, Illinois. His name occurs on maps of the Kaibab Plateau as DeMotte Park.

[34] John Doyle Lee, *A Mormon Chronicle, The Diaries of John D. Lee, 1848-1876*, edited and annotated by Robert Glass Cleland and Juanita Brooks (San Marino, Calif.: Huntington Library, 1955), vol. II, p. 208.

[35] E.O. Beaman was the first photographer of the Powell Colorado River Survey. He was a professional out of the state of New York, and he was hired by Powell upon recommendation of an outstanding photographic supply house in New York City. Beaman made approximately 350 negatives while in Powell's service. He saw photography in the West as a lucrative enterprise for himself and left Powell's service in January of 1872. The parting was not altogether amicable. Beaman, in his private venture, went on to take some early pictures of Grand Canyon and the Hopi villages.

[36] James Fennemore (1849-1941), the last survivor of the Powell Colorado River Expedition died at Phoenix, Arizona, January 25, 1941, at the age of ninety-one. During the fall of 1871, Major Powell met Fennemore at a photography shop in Salt Lake City. Fennemore was an assistant in the shop of Charles R. Savage's gallery, and he made the prints from Beaman's stereoscopic negatives in order that Powell might take them to Washington when he appealed for additional appropriations for his exploration (William Culp Darrah, *Utah Historical Quarterly*, vol. XVI-XVII [1948-1949]).

[37] Sarah Caroline Williams, fourth wife of John D. Lee, was born November 24, 1830,

in Murfreesboro, Tennessee. She was married to Lee on April 19, 1845, in Nauvoo, Illinois, and had eleven children by him. She died on February 16, 1907 in Torrey, Utah (Juanita Brooks, *John Doyle Lee, Zealot-Pioneer Builder-Scapegoat*).

[38] John Doyle Lee, *A Mormon Chronicle, The Diaries of John D. Lee, 1848-1876*, edited and annotated by Robert Glass Cleland and Juanita Brooks (San Marino, Calif.: Huntington Library, 1955), vol. II, pp. 219-20.

[39] *Ibid.*, p. 236.

[40] *Ibid.*, p. 238.

[41] *Ibid.*, p. 192.

[42] *Ibid.*, p. 327-28.

[43] *Ibid.*, p. 381.

[44] *Ibid.*, p. 383.

[45] *Ibid.*, p. 447.

[46] *Ibid.*, p. 380.

[47] Juanita Brooks, *The Mountain Meadows Massacre* (Stanford: Stanford University Press, 1950), p. 82.

[48] John Doyle Lee, *A Mormon Chronicle, The Diaries of John D. Lee, 1848-1876*, edited and annotated by Robert Glass Cleland and Juanita Brooks (San Marino, Calif.: Huntington Library, 1955), vol. II, p. 147.

[49] Walter Clement (Clem) Powell (1850-1883) was first cousin of Major John Wesley Powell. An orphan, he was raised in the home of the Reverend Joseph Powell (the Major's father and a Methodist minister). With the Colorado Survey party, he was assistant on the photographic exploits of Beaman and later of Hillers. He later became associated with the wholesale drug and tobacco business in Omaha. Married, with one daughter, he died at the age of thirty-three (Charles Kelly: *Utah Historical Quarterly*, vols. XVI-XVII, and Wallace Stegner, *Beyond The Hundredth Meridian*).

[50] Charles Kelly, (ed.), "Walter Clement Powell," *Utah Historical Quarterly*, vols. XVI-XVII (1948-49), p. 470.

[51] The Hafens, in *Handcarts to Zion* refer to it as "the most remarkable travel experiment in the history of Western America. Nearly three thousand men, women and children, pulling their worldly possessions in hand-made, two-wheeled carts, trudged some thirteen hundred miles to the Zion of their hopes" (*Handcarts to Zion, The Story of a Unique Western Migration, 1856-1860, Far West and Rockies Series*, vol. XIV, by Leroy R. Hafen and Ann W. Hafen, "Foreword").
Note: The handcarts were furnished by the church. Supply wagons with the handcart "trains" carried food for the journey.

[52] Story: Miss Sharlot M. Hall, Arizona Territorial Historian, portion of her diary published in *Arizona Highways*, 1912. Also James H. McClintock, *Mormon Settlement in Arizona* (Phoenix, Ariz., 1921).

[53] The Southern Pacific Railroad was completed to the Colorado in Yuma, Arizona, in 1877 (E.C. LaRue, *Colorado River and Its Utilization, Water Supply Paper 395*, p. 20).

[54] James H. McClintock, *Mormon Settlement in Arizona* (Phoenix, Arizona: 1921), p. 95.

[55] The Southern Pacific Railroad was completed to the Colorado at Yuma, Arizona in 1877. The Atlantic and Pacific crossed the Colorado at Needles in 1883. The Rio Grande Western crossed the Green in Gunnison Valley, Utah, in 1883, and the Union Pacific had been constructed to Green River, Wyoming, in 1869 (E.C. LaRue, *The Colorado and Its Utilization, Water Supply Paper 395*).

[56] Frank Mason Brown was a prominent Denver businessman who was interested in the Denver, Colorado Canyon and Pacific Railroad as a project for investment purposes and

as such made considerable advances of money to determine the engineering feasibility of the project. When the company for the railroad survey was formed in 1889, Brown was elected president.

[57] James Gillespie Blaine (1830-1893), a Pennsylvanian by birth, settled in Maine where he became a political leader, serving the state as both a representative and a senator. He was one of the founders of the Republican Party and was presented by Robert Ingersoll as a candidate for president the same year Rutherford B. Hayes, governor of Ohio, won that nomination on the seventh ballot. In the political arenas of his time, he was known as The Plumed Knight.

[58] Robert Brewster Stanton (1846-1922), a Mississippian by birth, was the son of a prominent Presbyterian minister who later became president of Miami University in Oxford, Ohio. Stanton graduated from this University in 1871. Though his educational background was a classical one, he had worked with a railroad survey party during a summer vacation and decided to be a civil engineer. His first work west was with the Atlantic and Pacific Railroad. Continuing his surveying and construction work with railroad lines, he became interested in mining and gained stature in that field also. He was chief engineer on the Denver, Colorado Canyon and Pacific Railroad Survey. Later he traveled to all parts of the world in the capacity of civil and mining engineer. He was considered a fine lecturer and was in demand on the circuits. He was a meticulous researcher and was a learned historian of the Colorado River and always considered his work there as his meaningful years.

[59] Franklin A. Nims, was the photographer with the Brown-Stanton party. "Biographical data on Nims is scarce." This is from one of the Denver newspapers about the time of his work with the Stanton party. "Mr. Nims is about 30 years of age, and is a photographer and newspaper man by profession. He is a native of Eldorado, Kansas, but came to Denver a little over a year ago...." The above summation, including the quotations, is from the "Foreword" of *The Photographer and the River* edited by Dwight L. Smith, p. 16.

[60] Franklin A. Nims, *The Photographer and the River, 1889-1890, The Colorado Cañon Diary of Franklin A. Nims,* edited by Dwight L. Smith (Santa Fe: Stagecoach Press, 1967), p. 36.

[61] *Ibid.*

[62] *Ibid.,* p. 37.

[63] *Ibid.,* p. 37.

[64] *Ibid.,* p. 37.

[65] *Ibid.,* pp. 37-38.

[66] *Ibid.,* p. 37.

[67] *Ibid.,* p. 37.

[68] *Ibid.,* p. 37.

[69] Robert Brewster Stanton, *Down The Colorado,* edited with an introduction by Dwight L. Smith (Norman: University of Oklahoma Press, 1965), pp. 108-09.

[70] Franklin A. Nims, *The Photographer and the River, 1889-1890, The Colorado Cañon Diary of Franklin A. Nims,* edited by Dwight L. Smith (Santa Fe: Stagecoach Press, 1967), p. 60.

[71] *Ibid.*

[72] Robert Brewster Stanton, *Down The Colorado,* edited with an introduction by Dwight L. Smith (Norman: University of Oklahoma Press, 1965), p. 115.

[73] *Ibid.* "...he had broken one of the bones in his leg just above the ankle."

[74] *Ibid.,* p. 112.

75 *Ibid.*, p. 117.

76 *Ibid.*, p. 117.

77 *Ibid.*, p. 227.

78 Captain Pardyn Dodds, U.S. Army, (sometimes also spelled Pardon), was stationed at "Fort Uintah" of the Uinta Indian Agency (Wallace Stegner, *Beyond The Hundredth Meridian* and others).

79 In March 1880, the Navajo Indians killed "James Merrick and Ernest Mitchell in Monument Valley. The two were in search of a hidden mine believed to be the source of the silver used by the Indians in their jewelry. When a searching party found some samples of silver ore with the bodies it was thought the prospectors had located the mine. Although no one after them ever found out where the samples of ore came from, the Merrick-Mitchell mine was a lodestone for prospectors who searched for it in the Monument Valley-Navajo Mountain region for at least five years" (C. Gregory Crampton, "Historic Glen Canyon," *Utah Historical Quarterly*, vol. XXVIII, No. 3, July 1960, p. 282).

80 Dandy Crossing at the mouth of Trachyte Creek. It was the principal Indian Crossing between Green River, Utah, and the Crossing of the Fathers. It was also a part of a Mormon wagon road from central Utah to Bluff, on the San Juan River (H.E. Gregory, notes from Diary of Almon Harris Thompson, *Utah Historical Quarterly*, vol. VII, 1939, p. 54).

81 From "Colorado River Gold" by Cass Hite, *Utah Historical Quarterly*, vol. VII, 1939, pp. 13-140. originally in *Beaver Utonian*, January 13, 1893.

82 Franklin A. Nims, *The Photographer and the River 1889-1890, The Colorado Cañon Diary of Franklin A. Nims*, edited by Dwight L. Smith (Santa Fe: Stage Coach Press, 1967), p. 33.

83 *Ibid.*, p. 36.

84 *Ibid.*, p. 36.

85 *Ibid.*, p. 36.

86 John Colton Sumner (1840-1907) was born in Indiana, but his family migrated westward first to Illinois and then to Iowa. He was raised on a farm, but was known as a good marksman and a good boatman. Sumner served three years in the War Between the States. He then moved to Denver where some of his family had relocated. Starting his own outfitting business in Middle Park, Colorado, it was here he met Powell who had a letter of introduction from a mutual friend. Sumner served with Powell's first expedition and went on down to Fort Yuma after the group was disbanded. After that he returned to commercial hunting, later moving to Wyoming and then to Grand Junction, Colorado, where he worked with placers. He is buried in Denver, Colorado. (William Culp Darrah, *Utah Historical Quarterly*, vol. XV, 1947, pp. 109-112).

87 Robert Brewster Stanton, "The Hoskaninni Papers, Mining in Glen Canyon, 1897-1902," edited by C. Gregory Crampton and Dwight L. Smith, University of Utah, Department of Anthropology, *Anthropological Papers*, Number 54 (Glen Canyon Series Number 15), November (Salt Lake City: University of Utah Press, 1961), p. xii "Introduction."

88 *Ibid.*, p. 37.

89 "Hoskaninni commemorates a Navajo Chief by that name who had befriended Cass Hite; the Indian's name is usually spelled Hoskininni. Before coming to Glen Canyon in 1883 Hite had been prospecting in the Navajo country where he was looking for the lost Merrick-Mitchell mine. He gave up the search when the Chief told him that gold could be found along the Colorado River. Stanton, who is undoubtedly responsible for the name, must have heard of Hoskaninni from Cass Hite, whom he met in Glen Canyon during the railroad survey" (C. Gregory Crampton, "Historical Sites in Glen Canyon,

Mouth of Hansen Creek to Mouth of San Juan River," University of Utah, Department of Anthropology, *Anthropological Papers,* Number 61, (Glen Canyon Series Number 17), December [Salt Lake City: University of Utah Press, 1962], p. 62).

[90] C. Gregory Crampton, "Historical Sites in Glen Canyon, Mouth of San Juan to Lee's Ferry," University of Utah, Department of Anthropology, *Anthropological Papers,* Number 46 (Glen Canyon Series Number 12), June (Salt Lake City: University of Utah Press, 1960), p. 74.

[91] C. Gregory Crampton, "Outline History of the Glen Canyon Region 1776-1922." University of Utah, Department of Anthropology, *Anthropological Papers,* Number 42 (Glen Canyon Series Number 9), September (Salt Lake City: University of Utah Press, 1959), p. 31.

[92] *Ibid.,* pp. 31-32.

[93] Robert B. Stanton, "The Hoskaninni Papers, Mining in Glen Canyon, 1897-1902," edited by C. Gregory Crampton and Dwight L. Smith, University of Utah, Department of Anthropology, *Anthropological Papers,* Number 54 (Glen Canyon Series Number 15), November (Salt Lake City: University of Utah Press, 1961), pp. 50-51.

[94] *Ibid.,* p. 50.

[95] Robert B. Stanton, "The Hoskaninni Papers, Mining in Glen Canyon, 1897-1902," edited by C. Gregory Crampton and Dwight L. Smith, University of Utah, Department of Anthropology, *Anthropological Papers,* Number 54 (Glen Canyon Series Number 15), November (Salt Lake City: University of Utah Press, 1961), pp. 104-05.

[96] C. Gregory Crampton, "Historical Sites in Glen Canyon, Mouth of San Juan to Lee's Ferry," University of Utah, Department of Anthropology, *Anthropological Papers,* Number 46 (Glen Canyon Series Number 12), June (Salt Lake City: University of Utah Press, 1960), pp. 86-87.

[97] C. Gregory Crampton, "The San Juan Canyon Historical Sites," University of Utah, Department of Anthropology, *Anthropological Papers,* Number 70 (Glen Canyon Series Number 22), June (Salt Lake City: University of Utah Press, 1964), p. 44.

[98] C. Gregory Crampton, "Historical Sites in Glen Canyon, Mouth of San Juan to Lee's Ferry," University of Utah, Department of Anthropology, *Anthropological Papers,* Number 46 (Glen Canyon Series Number 12), June (Salt Lake City: University of Utah Press, 1960), pp. 87-88.

[99] Ellsworth L. Kolb, *Through the Grand Canyon from Wyoming to Mexico* (New York, The Macmillan Company, 1914), p. 171.

[100] *Ibid.,* p. 172.

[101] Emery and Ellsworth Kolb had come to the south rim of Grand Canyon around 1900 and established a photography studio there. They, however, did more than take pictures of tourists to the area, for it did not take them long to become enamored of the beauty of the canyon and to begin a photographic study of it. Their dream was to do a photographic record of the Colorado itself. With them on their trip they had a motion picture camera. They wanted to "bring out a record of the Colorado as it is, a live thing, armed as it were with teeth, ready to crush and devour." Ellsworth L. Kolb wrote about this trip in his book *Through the Grand Canyon from Wyoming to Mexico.* The quotation is from his book, p. 4.

[102] Ellsworth L. Kolb, *Through the Grand Canyon from Wyoming to Mexico* (New York· The Macmillan Company, 1914), p. 173.

[103] *Ibid.*

[104] *Ibid.,* p. 174.

[105] *Ibid.,* p. 179.

[106] *Ibid.,* pp. 179-80.

[107] C. Gregory Crampton, "Historical Sites in Glen Canyon, Mouth of San Juan to Lee's Ferry," University of Utah, Department of Anthropology, *Anthropological Papers,* Number 46 (Glen Canyon Series Number 12), June (Salt Lake City: University of Utah Press, 1960), pp. 87-88.

[108] *Ibid.*

[109] "The bridge itself was no small engineering feat. It is located 130 miles north of Flagstaff, Arizona, the nearest railroad point, 6 miles downstream from Lee's Ferry, and about 70 miles southwest of Kanab, Utah. The cantilever structural steel design was adopted because it was found that the suspension type of bridge was impracticable. Fifteen thousand tons of materials hauled over atrociously rough roads in trucks were needed. The main span of the bridge is 616 feet long and its 18 foot roadbed is 467 feet above the low water level of the bridge. Including abutments, the bridge is 834 feet long. To defray costs of construction, Congress appropriated $100,000 and Arizona $285,000" (Leland Hargrave Creer, "Mormon Towns in the Region of the Colorado," University of Utah, *Anthropological Papers,* Number 32 (Glen Canyon Series Number 3), May, 1958, p. 24).

[110] James H. McClintock, *Mormon Settlement in Arizona* (Phoenix, Arizona, 1921).

[111] Wilford Woodruff, 1807-1898, was born in Connecticut. He became a member of the L.D.S. Church at the age of twenty-six, was a missionary in the southern part of the United States before going to the Fox Islands and England to serve the church. He came to Salt Lake Valley with the Pioneer Company in the summer of 1847. At the venerable age of eighty, he became president of the church.

[112] George Wharton James, *In and Around the Grand Canyon* (Cambridge: University Press, John Wilson and Son, 1900), pp. 221-22. Lee never returned to the Paria after he was arrested in Panguitch, Utah, on November 7, 1874, 23 years before Wharton was at the ferry. James S. Emmett was the ferryman at the time of Wharton's visit.

[113] *Ibid.,* p. 235.
George Wharton James, September 27, 1858-November 8, 1923, died while on a lecture tour in Saint Helen, California. A prolific writer, some of James' books are as follows:
Arizona, the Wonderland
The Grand Canyon of Arizona
How to Make Indian and Other Baskets
In and Around the Grand Canyon
Indian Basketry
Indian Blankets and Their Makers
New Mexico, The Land of the Delight Makers
Our American Wonderlands
The Wonders of The Colorado Desert

[114] William Henry Ashley, a Virginian, emigrated to Missouri, became a general of the Territorial militia and was later a congressman from Missouri. He went into the fur trade in 1822.

[115] Bullboats were made of buffalo skins sewn together and stretched over a frame of willow or cottonwood poles. Their normal dimensions were about thirty feet long, with a twelve foot beam and a draft of twenty inches. The sewn buffalo skins were smeared with pitch.

[116] Julius F. Stone, *Canyon Country, The Romance of a Drop of Water and A Grain of Sand* (New York: G.P. Putnam's Sons, 1932), p. 82.

[117] *Ibid.,* p. 67.

[118] C. Gregory Crampton, "Historical Sites in Glen Canyon, Mouth of San Juan to Lee's Ferry," University of Utah, Department of Anthropology, *Anthropological Papers,* Number 46 (Glen Canyon Series Number 12), June (Salt Lake City: University of Utah Press, 1960), p. 90.

[119] Julius F. Stone, *Canyon Country, The Romance of a Drop of Water and A Grain of Sand* (New York: G.P. Putnam's Sons, 1932), p. 107.

[120] *Ibid.,* p. 107.

Note: Stone's sadness was somewhat premature. He was back on the river again and again, the last time when he was eighty-three (*see* photograph, page 80, courtesy of the National Park Service). Stone died in 1947 at the age of ninety-two. He always had strong, positive feelings about the Colorado and the time he had spent on it.

[121] Frank Gruber, *Zane Grey* (Cleveland: The World Publishing Company, 1970), p. 65.

[122] *Ibid.,* p. 69.

[123] *The Coconino Sun,* Flagstaff, Arizona, vol. XXIV, No. 15, Thursday, April 11, 1907, p. 1.

[124] *The Coconino Sun,* Flagstaff, Arizona, vol. XXIV, No. 16, Thursday, April 18, 1907, p. 1.

[125] *Ibid.*

[126] Frank Gruber, *Zane Grey* (Cleveland: The World Publishing Company, 1970), p. 70.

[127] *Ibid.,* p. 71.

The Last of The Plainsmen was first published by the Outing Publishing Company in 1908, but Grey was to receive money from it only if it went into a second printing. Later, A.C. McClurg, a reprint house, brought it out in a low-priced edition. Gruber, Grey's biographer, said it eventually earned about two hundred dollars for Grey (*Ibid.,* pp. 80-81).

[128] James A. Little, *Jacob Hamblin in Three Mormon Classics,* compiled by Preston Nibley (Salt Lake City: Stevens & Wallis, Inc., 1944), p. 296.

[129] J.W. Powell, *Exploration of the Colorado River of the West* (Washington, D.C.: Government Printing Office, 1875), p. 320.

[130] Robert M. Utley, "The Reservation Trader in Navajo History," *El Palacio,* Spring 1961, p. 7.

[131] Richard F. Van Valkenburgh, *Diné Bikéyah,* edited by Lucy Wilcox Adams and John C. McPhee, Mimeo, (Window Rock, Arizona, 1941), p. 103.

Frank McNitt, in his book, *The Indian Traders* (Norman: University of Oklahoma Press, Second Printing, August 1963), p. 98, gives the spelling as follows: *Ha'naant'eetiin,* "Crossing Against the Current," *Tsinaa'ee dahsi'áni,* "Where the Boat Sits."

[132] In connection with Queen Victoria's Jubilee, "American Promoters organized 'An Exhibition of the Arts, Industries, Manufactures, Products and Resources of the United States,' commonly known as the American Exhibition. Prime movers in this project were Colonel Henry S. Russell, President; John Robinson Whitley, Director General; and Vincent Applin, Secretary. They offered their facilities and a percentage of the gate receipts to Cody and Salsbury for Buffalo Bill's Wild West as a feature of their program. The partners accepted" (Donald Bert Russell, *The Lives and Legends of Buffalo Bill* [Norman: University of Oklahoma Press, 1960], p. 323).

[133] John Burke, *Buffalo Bill, The Noblest Whiteskin* (New York: G.P. Putnam's Sons, 1973), pp. 173-74.

[134] Major Andrew Sheridan Burt "enlisted as a private in the Sixth Ohio Volunteer Infantry in 1861 and within a month was commissioned first lieutenant in the Eighteenth U.S. Infantry. He was brevetted captain for gallantry at Mill Spring and major for the Atlanta campaign and Jonesboro, and was captain in the Ninth U.S. Infantry at the time he became a dramatist. Subsequently he became brigadier general of volunteers in the Spanish-American War and attained that rank in the Regular Army in 1902" (Donald Bert Russell, *The Lives and Legends of Buffalo Bill* [Norman: University of Oklahoma Press, 1960], p. 259).

[135] *Ibid.,* p. 259.

[136] *The Coconino Weekly Sun,* #9, vol. X, Thursday, November 10, 1892, p. 3, column 4, states the group stayed at the Del Monte Hotel. Members of the party are listed as: Col. Cody, Major Mildway (English Army), Col. McKinnon, Prentiss Ingraham (English), Major John Burk, Capt. W.H. Broach, H.S. Boal and businessmen from the East. Captain John Hance, in his own words as "guide, story-teller and path-finder," in *Personal Impressions of the Grand Cañon of the Colorado River* (collected and compiled by G.K. Woods), published by the Whitaker & Ray Company, 1899, p. 63, listed on November 14, 1892, the Buffalo Bill Expedition to Grand Canyon as: W.F. Cody (Buffalo Bill); George P. Everhart, Chicago, Illinois; James T. Wells, Salt Lake City; Allison Nailor, Washington, D.C.; Frank D. Baldwin, John M. Burke, U.S. Army, H.S. Boal, North Platte, Nebraska; William D. Dowd, Flagstaff, A.T.; R.H. Haslam, Chicago, Illinois; E.C. Bradford, Denver, Colorado; W. Henry MacKinnon, England; W.H. Broach, North Platte, Nebraska; Daniel Seegmiller, Merritt S. Ingrahm, Washington, D.C. In small letters, the name Piper Heidsieck also appears on the November 14, 1892 register.

[137] Frank Waters, *The Colorado, The Rivers of America Series* (New York: Rinehart & Company, 1946), p. 414.

[138] *Ibid.,* p. 416.

[139] *Ibid.,* pp. 416-17.

[140] Otis Marston, "Fast Water," p. 68, from Wallace Stegner, (ed.), *This Is Dinosaur* (New York: Alfred A. Knopf, 1955).

[141] *Ibid.,* p. 69.

[142] Joseph Christmas Ives, Lieutenant, "Report Upon the Colorado River of the West," Executive Document No. 90, published by order of the Secretary of War, 1861, p. 110. Ives was a member of the Corps of Topographical Engineers. In the War Between the States he joined the Confederacy and became a member of Jefferson Davis' personal staff. In his book, *Army Exploration in The American West, 1803-1863,* p. 19, William H. Goetzmann lists Ives as one of three officers who brought to their reports, "A kinship between science and art. . . . At their best they were able to express the west in qualitative terms."

[143] John A. Widtsoe (edited by A.R. Mortensen), "A Journal of John A. Widtsoe," *Utah Historical Quarterly,* vol. XXIII, Number 3, July 1955, pp. 195-231.

[144] P.T. Reilly, "How Deadly is Big Red," *Utah Historical Quarterly,* Volume 37, No. 2, Spring 1969, pp. 244-60.

[145] Edwin G. Woolley (edited by C. Gregory Crampton and David E. Miller), "Expedition to Intercept Navajoe Indians Who Had Stole Stock From Southern Utah, February 25 to March 12, 1869," in Journal of "Two Campaigns by The Utah Territorial Militia Against The Navajo Indian, 1869," *Utah Historical Quarterly,* vol. XXIX, No. 2, 1961, pp. 149-76. Quotation from p. 165.

[146] Gaylord Staveley, *Broken Waters Sing, Rediscovering Two Great Rivers of the West* (Boston: A Sports Illustrated Books, Little, Brown and Company, 1971), p. 194.

Bibliography

Books

Bailey, Paul. *Jacob Hamblin Buckskin Apostle.* Los Angeles: Westernlore Press, 1961.

Barnes, Will C. *Arizona Place Names.* Tucson: University of Arizona Press, 1935.

Beadle, J.H. *Western Wilds and The Men Who Redeem Them.* Cincinnati: Jones Brothers & Company, 1877.

Brooks, Juanita. *Emma Lee.* Logan: Utah State University Press, Western Text Society Series, 1975.

Brooks, Juanita. *John Doyle Lee (Zealot-Pioneer Builder-Scapegoat).* Glendale: The Arthur H. Clark Company, 1964. (Western Frontiersmen Series IX).

Brooks, Juanita. *The Mountain Meadows Massacre.* Stanford: Stanford University Press, 1950.

Burke, John. *Buffalo Bill, The Noblest Whiteskin.* New York: G.P. Putnam's Sons, 1973.

Corle, Edwin. *Listen, Bright Angel.* New York: Duell, Sloan and Pearce, 1946.

Chalfant, James M. *Colorado River Controversies.* New York: Dodd, Mead & Co., 1932.

Coues, Elliott. *On The Trail of a Spanish Pioneer, Garces Diary 1775-1776,* 2 volumes. New York: Francis P. Harper, 1900.

Dellenbaugh, Frederick S. *A Canyon Voyage.* New Haven: Yale University Press, 1908.

Dellenbaugh, Frederick S. *Romance of the Colorado River.* New York: G.P. Putnam's Sons, 1909.

Dellenbaugh, Frederick S. *Breaking the Wilderness.* New York: G.P. Putnam's Sons, 1905.

Freeman, Lewis R. *The Colorado River, Yesterday, Today and Tomorrow.* New York: Dodd, Mead and Company, 1923.

Granger, Byrd H. *Arizona Place Names,* Revised and Enlarged. Tucson: University of Arizona Press, 1960.

Gruber, Frank. *Zane Grey.* Cleveland: The World Publishing Company, 1970.

Hodge, Hiram C. *Arizona As It Was.* Chicago: The Rio Grande Press, 1962.

Ives, Joseph C., Lieut. *Report Upon The Colorado River of the West.* Executive Document No. 90, published by order of the Secretary of War, 1861.

James, George Wharton. *In and Around the Grand Canyon.* Cambridge: University Press, John Wilson and Son, 1900.

Kolb, Ellsworth L. *Through the Grand Canyon from Wyoming to Mexico.* New York: The Macmillan Company, 1914.

Lee, John Doyle. *A Mormon Chronicle.* The Diaries of John D. Lee, 1848-1876. Edited and annotated by Robert Glass Cleland and Juanita Brooks, 2 volumes. San Marino, California: Huntington Library, 1955.

Lee, John Doyle. *Mormonism Unveiled, or Life and Confessions of John D. Lee.* Edited by William W. Bishop. St. Louis: J.H. Mason, 1891.

Lee, Weston and Jeanne. *Torrent in the Desert.* Flagstaff, Arizona: Northland Press, 1962.

Leonard, Elizabeth Jane and Goodman, Julia Cody. Edited by James William Hoffman. *Buffalo Bill, King of the Old West.* New York: Library Publishers, 1955.

Lingenfelter, Richard E. *First Through The Grand Canyon.* Los Angeles: Glen Dawson, 1958.

Little, James A. *Jacob Hamblin in Three Mormon Classics,* compiled by Preston Nibley. Salt Lake City, Utah: Stevens & Wallis, Inc., 1944.

McClintock, James H. *Mormon Settlement in Arizona.* Phoenix, Arizona: 1921.

Malone, Dumas (ed.). *Dictionary of American Biography.* New York: Charles Scribner's Sons, 1935.

Marston, Otis Dock. "Fast Water" in *This is Dinosaur,* edited Wallace Earle Stegner. New York: Alfred A. Knopf, 1955.

McNitt, Frank. *The Indian Traders.* Norman: University of Oklahoma Press, 1962.

MaComb, Captain J.N. *Report of the Exploring Expedition from Santa Fe, New Mexico to the Junction of the Grand and Green Rivers of the Great Colorado of the West in 1859.* Department of U.S. Army, 1876.

MaComb, Captain J.N. *Report of the Exploring Expedition from Santa Fe, New Mexico to the Junction of the Grand and Green Rivers of the Great Colorado of the West, in 1859, Under Command of Captain J.N. MaComb, with a Geological Report by Professor J.S. Newberry.* Washington, D.C.: Government Printing Office, 1876.

Nims, Franklin A. *The Photographer and The River, 1889-1890.* The Colorado Cañon Diary of Franklin A. Nims, edited by Dwight L. Smith. Santa Fe: Stagecoach Press, 1967.

Peplow, Edward Hadduck. *History of Arizona,* 3 vols. New York: Lewis Historical Publishing Company, 1958.

Powell, J.W. *Exploration of the Colorado River of the West.* Washington, D.C.: Government Printing Office, 1875.

Prudden, T. Mitchell. *On the Great American Plateau.* New York: G.P. Putnam's Sons, 1906.

Russell, Donald Bert. *The Lives and Legends of Buffalo Bill.* Norman: University of Oklahoma Press, 1960.

Stanton, Robert Brewster. *Down The Colorado,* edited with an introduction by Dwight L. Smith. Norman: University of Oklahoma Press, 1965.

Staveley, Gaylord. *Broken Waters Sing, Rediscovering Two Great Rivers of the*

West. Boston: A Sports Illustrated Book, Little Brown and Company, 1971.

Stegner, Wallace E. *Beyond the Hundredth Meridian: John Wesley Powell and the Second Opening of the West.* Boston: Houghton Mifflin, 1954.

Stegner, Wallace (ed.). *This is Dinosaur.* New York: Alfred A. Knopf, 1955.

Stone, Julius F. *Canyon Country, The Romance of A Drop of Water and A Grain of Sand.* New York: G.P. Putnam's Sons, 1932.

Van Valkenburgh, Richard F. *Diné Bikéyah,* edited by Lucy Wilcox Adams and John C. McPhee (Mimeo). Window Rock, Arizona, 1941.

Waters, Frank. *The Colorado, The Rivers of America Series.* New York: Rinehart & Company, 1946.

Wyllys, Rufus Kay. *Arizona, The History of a Frontier State.* Phoenix: Hobson & Herr, 1950.

Watkins, T.H. and Contributors. *The Grand Colorado, The Story of a River and its Canyons.* American West Publishing Co., 1969.

Periodicals

Auerbach, Herbert S. (Translator). "Journal and Itinerary of the Reverend Fathers Fray Francisco Atanasio Dominguez and Fray Silvestre Velez de Escalante Concerning the Discovery of the Route from Presidio de Santa Fe del Nuevo Mexico to Monterey in Northern California." *Utah Historical Quarterly,* vol. XI, No. 1, 2, 3, 4, January, April, July, October 1943, pp. 27-113.

Brooks, Juanita. "Jest a Copyin' Word f'r Word." *Utah Historical Quarterly,* vol. 37, No. 4, Fall 1969, pp. 375-95.

Crampton, C. Gregory. "Historic Glen Canyon." *Utah Historical Quarterly,* vol. XXVIII, No. 3, July 1960, pp. 275-89.

Alexander, Thomas G. and Arrington, Leonard J. "The Utah Military Frontier, 1872-1912, Forts Cameron, Thornburgh and Duchesne." *Utah Historical Quarterly,* vol. XXXII, No. 4, Fall 1964, pp. 330-39.

Bolton, Herbert E. "Pageant in the Wilderness," The Story of the Escalante Expedition to the Interior Basin, 1776 (including the Diary and Itinerary of Father Escalante, Translated and Annotated); also Miera's Report. *Utah Historical Quarterly,* vol. XVIII, No. 1, 2, 3, 4, January, April, July and October 1950.

Brooks, Juanita. "Lee's Ferry at Lonely Dell," *Utah Historical Quarterly,* vol. XXV, No. 4, October, 1957, pp. 283-95.

Darrah, William Culp. "The Colorado River Expedition of 1869." *Utah Historical Quarterly,* Volume XV, No. 1, 2, 3, 4, 1947, pp. 9-18.

Darrah, William Culp. "Major Powell Prepares for a Second Expedition." *Utah Historical Quarterly,* vol. XV, No. 1, 2, 3, 4, 1947, pp. 149-153.

Darrah, William Culp. "Beaman, Fennemore, Hillers, Dellenbaugh, Johnson and Hattan," *Utah Historical Quarterly,* vols. XVI, No. 1, and XVII, No. 1, 2, 3, 4, 1949, pp. 491-503.

Darrah, William Culp. "J.C. Sumner's Journal," *Utah Historical Quarterly,* vol. XV, No. 1, 2, 3, 4, January, April, July, October 1947, pp. 113-24.

Darrah, William Culp (ed.). "John F. Steward." *Utah Historical Quarterly,* vols. XVI-XVII (1948-1949), pp. 175-251.

Darrah, William Culp (ed.). "John C. Sumner." *Utah Historical Quarterly,* vol. XV, 1947, pp. 109-24.

Darrah, William Culp. "Walter Henry Powell." *Utah Historical Quarterly,* vol. XV, 1947, p. 89.

Darrah, William Culp (ed.). "Hawkins, Hall, and Goodman." *Utah Historical Quarterly,* vol. XV, 1947, pp. 106-08.

Darrah, William Culp (ed.). "George Young Bradley's Journal," *Utah Historical Quarterly,* vol. XV, 1947, pp. 31-72.

Gregory, Herbert E. (ed.). "Diary of Almon Harris Thompson," *Utah Historical Quarterly,* vol. VII, No. 1, 2, 3, January, April, July 1939, pp. 5-140.

Gregory, Herbert E. (ed.). "Stephen Vandeveer Jones," *Utah Historical Quarterly,* vols. XVI-XVII (1948-1949) pp. 11-174.

Jennings, Jesse D. and Sharrock, Floyd W. "The Glen Canyon: A Multi-Discipline Project." *Utah Historical Quarterly,* vol. XXXIII, No. 1, Winter 1965, pp. 35-50.

Kelly, Charles (ed.). "Captain Francis Marion Bishop's Journal." *Utah Historical Quarterly,* vol. XV, 1947, pp. 159-253.

Kelly, Charles (ed.). "Walter Clement Powell." *Utah Historical Quarterly,* vols. XVI-XVII, 1948-49, pp. 253-490.

Kolb, E.L. "River Running, 1921, The Diary of E.L. Kolb," edited by W.L. Rusho. *Utah Historical Quarterly,* vol. XXXVII, Spring 1969, No. 2, pp. 269-83.

Marston, Otis. "River Runners: Fast Water Navigation." *Utah Historical Quarterly,* vol. XXVIII, No. 3, July 1960, pp. 291-308.

Reilly, P.T. "How Deadly Is Big Red." *Utah Historical Quarterly,* vol. XXXVII, No. 2, Spring 1969, pp. 244-60.

Report of death of George Wharton James. *El Palacio,* Volume XV, No. 11, December 1, 1923, p. 184.

Rusho, W.L. "Living History at Lee's Ferry." *Journal of the West,* Volume VII, No. 1, January 1968, pp. 64-75.

Rusho, W.L. (ed.). "River Running 1921: The Diary of E.L. Kolb." *Utah Historical Quarterly,* Spring, 1969, vol. XXXVII, No. 2, pp. 269-83.

Utah Historical Quarterly, volumes XV, XVI, XVII, Letters of members of expedition to various eastern newspapers.

Utley, Robert M. "The Reservation Trader in Navajo History." *El Palacio,* Spring 1961, p. 5.

Widtsoe, John A. (ed. by A.R. Mortensen). "A Journal of John A. Widtsoe." *Utah Historical Quarterly,* vol. XXIII, Number 3, July 1955, pp. 195-231.

Woodbury, Angus M. "A History of Southern Utah and Its National Parks." *Utah Historical Quarterly,* vol. XII, July-October 1944, No. 3-4, pp. 111-209.

Woolley, Edwin G. (edited by C. Gregory Crampton and David E. Miller). "Expedition to Intercept Navajoe Indians Who Had Stolen Stock from Southern Utah, February 25 to March 12, 1869," in "Journal of Two Campaigns by The Utah Territorial Militia Against the Navajo Indians,

1869." *Utah Historical Quarterly,* vol. XXIX, No. 2, April 1961, pp. 149-76.

Anthropological Papers

Creer, Leland Hargrave. "The Activities of Jacob Hamblin In The Region of the Colorado." *University of Utah Anthropological Papers,* No. 33 (Glen Canyon Series Number 3), May 1958.

LaRue, E.C. "Colorado River and Its Utilization," *Water Supply Paper 395,* Washington, D.C.: U.S. Government Printing Office, 1916.

Crampton, C. Gregory. "Historical Sites in Glen Canyon Mouth of San Juan to Lee's Ferry." University of Utah, Department of Anthropology, *Anthropological Papers,* No. 46 (Glen Canyon Series Number 12), June 1960. Salt Lake City: University of Utah Press. Charles E. Dibble, editor.

Crampton, C. Gregory. "Historical Sites in Glen Canyon, Mouth of Hansen Creek to Mouth of San Juan River." University of Utah, Department of Anthropology, *Anthropological Papers,* No. 61 (Glen Canyon Series Number 17), December 1962. Salt Lake City: University of Utah Press.

Crampton, C. Gregory. "The San Juan Canyon Historical Sites." University of Utah, Department of Anthropology, *Anthropological Papers,* No. 70 (Glen Canyon Series Number 22), June 1964. Salt Lake City: University of Utah Press.

Crampton, C. Gregory. "Outline History of the Glen Canyon Region, 1776-1922," University of Utah, Department of Anthropology, *Anthropological Papers,* No. 42, (Glen Canyon Series Number 9), September 1959. Salt Lake City: University of Utah Press.

Creer, Leland Hargrave. "Mormon Towns in the Region of the Colorado." *University of Utah Anthropological Papers,* No. 32 (Glen Canyon Series Number 3), May 1958. Salt Lake City: University of Utah Press.

Gregory, Herbert E. "The Navajo Country: A Geographic and Hydrographic Reconnaissance of Parts of Arizona, New Mexico and Utah," *Water Supply Paper No. 380.* Washington, D.C.: U.S. Government Printing Office, 1916.

Stanton, Robert B. "The Hoskaninni Papers, Mining in Glen Canyon, 1897-1902." Edited by C. Gregory Crampton and Dwight L. Smith, University of Utah, Department of Anthropology, *Anthropological Papers,* No. 54 (Glen Canyon Series Number 15), November 1961. Salt Lake City: University of Utah Press.

Newspapers

The Coconino Weekly Sun, Flagstaff, Arizona, vol. X, no. 9, p. 3, column 4, Thursday, November 10, 1892.

Coconino County Sun, Flagstaff, Arizona, vol. X, no. 15, p. 2, column 3, Thursday, December 27, 1892.

The Coconino Sun, Flagstaff Arizona:

    vol. XXIV, no. 15, p. 1, April 11, 1907;

    vol. XXIV, no. 16, p. 1, Thursday, April 18, 1907.

Santa Fe New Mexican, Santa Fe, New Mexico:

    vol. IX, no. 889, p. 1, column 4, paragraph 3, March 24, 1877;

    vol. no. 65, no. 144, p. 1, column 5 and 6, p. 4, column 4 and 5, June 17, 1929 (Byline: E. Dana Johnson).

Index